Forex And Crypto 2021:

Make Money Trading Online With The

$11,000 per Month Guide

(2 Books In 1)

David Uchiha

TABLE OF CONTENTS

Forex 2021:

The Best Methods For Forex

Trading.

Make Money Trading Online With The $11,000 per Month

Guide

Forex and Cryptocurrency 2021:
The Best Methods For Forex and Crypto
Trading.
Make Money Trading Online With The $11,000 per Month Guide

INTRODUCTION

Welcome to the beginning of this journey. In this book, we are going to explore the FOREX market and what it represents for investors all over the world. This book has been written with the novice investor in mind. As such, we will be covering the basics of FOREX, how you can get into the market, and how you can make the most out of your investments. Best of all, we will be presenting all of this in an easy to digest format. Sure, we are going to be covering some rather technical terminology. Nevertheless, we'll make sure that you get the information you need in a way that resonates with you.

This book is for all of those folks who are looking to get into the FOREX market but don't really know how to go about it. This is why each chapter focuses specifically on an aspect related to currency markets and how you can benefit from placing your money in FOREX. The main thing to keep in mind is that you can make sustainable gains by following the guidelines that we present. In this manner, you can be sure that you won't lose out on the deals you make.

In addition, please bear in mind that investing in financial markets always poses a risk. After all, there are no sure deals. Every time you enter a trade, you can expect to carry some degree of risk. This is important to note as you can't always expect to make massive profits. In fact, highly successful FOREX investors make money by multiplying minor deals over and over again. When you are able to do this, you will find that making a consistent return on your deals is far easier than you might have thought.

So, what are you waiting for?

Let's begin on the journey that will lead you from the couch to FOREX investment success. While it does take some time and effort to master the overall scheme of the FOREX market, you will find that this guide will provide you with all of the essentials you need to hit the ground running. You won't have to scour the internet to find a credible source of information. Everything you need is right here.

Please bear in mind that making money in FOREX is based on the time and effort you are willing to put into the research needed to place successful deals. The good news is that this guide will provide you with the guidelines you need to make successful trades. While you may not win every single time, you can rest assured that you will come out on top, most of the time.

That's where the real money is made.

One last thing: we ask that you read through this guide to the end before placing your first trades. It's essential that you gain an understanding of the entire scope of FOREX trading prior to getting started. That way, you can be sure that you won't make any initial mistakes that could cost you lots of money.

Let's get on with it!

CHAPTER 1

Introduction To Forex Trading

FOREX is a financial market that deals in currency trading exclusively. Now, please don't be confused with other financial markets, such as the stock market. Stocks are completely different types of financial investments that don't have a direct relation with FOREX. This is why we will spend the length of this book discussing currencies.

It's important to keep in mind that currency refers to the type of money that every country issues. This is the underlying fundamental tenet of FOREX. We are talking about comparing the valuation of each country's currency as it relates to another. As such, you need to understand that money and currency are two different things.

In general, money can be any commodity known to man. Historically, several commodities have served as money, such as salt, feathers, cocoa beans, and cattle. However, gold and silver became the main commodities that have served as money throughout history.

The reason why gold and silver are not currency any longer is due to the fact that they are in short supply. It can be tough and expensive to mine gold and silver out of the ground. Therefore, our modern economy needed to find another commodity that could serve as money while ensuring the growth of a modern economy.

This is where the modern currencies we know today come into play. Depending on the country you live in, you will be dealing with one currency or another. Also, depending on your lifestyle, you may be dealing with multiple currencies. In that case, you can appreciate the interaction that goes on among multiple currencies while also understanding the valuation that exists among different currencies.

As a result, buying and selling currencies is a natural occurrence in modern financial markets. Of course, you don't need to become a big-time investor to take part in this type of market. A very simple example of how you can participate in currency trading is when you travel. When you exchange your country's currency for that of the country you are visiting, you have placed a currency exchange trade. The main difference is that such transactions don't have speculative purposes.

This is an important thing to note here.

Speculation refers to the motivation behind making trades. When you place a trade for speculative purposes, you are doing so with the hope of making money on another trade later on. In other words, you are looking to buy low and sell high just as you would with stocks, bonds, or any other type of financial asset.

Throughout this book, we will be discussing currency pairs. In order for a FOREX trade to take place, you need to become familiar with the various types of currency pairs that are commonly traded. When you have pairs that are commonly traded, such as the Euro and the US Dollar, we call these "correlated pairs." These pairs usually have the highest trade volume and offer you the best opportunity to make money.

By the same token, you can place trades in "uncorrelated pairs," meaning that they don't have a direct relation to one another. In such cases, the trades are riskier but can offer a great deal of potential profits.

This is why it's important to fully understand the dynamics of the FOREX market so that you can make the best investment decisions based on your expectations and investment strategy.

Types of FOREX Markets

There are various types of FOREX markets you can choose to invest in. Depending on your expectations, experience, and interests, you can choose to invest in any of these markets. The best part of all is that you can dip your toes into all markets at the same time. However, we don't recommend this right away. It's always best to master one market before moving on to the next. Eventually, you'll be able to make money in various types of markets at the same time.

Also, please keep in mind that understand how each market works is both a question of practice and experience. So, it's always a good idea to study the dynamics of each market. That way, when you are set to market some money, you know what to expect. Moreover, you'll be ready for anything that might come your way.

The Spot Market

By far, this is the most common market within the FOREX domain. The reason why it's called "spot" it's because the transactions which take place in this market happen at the current exchange rate. Please bear in mind that exchange rates vary all the time. Therefore, you need to keep a close eye on where they are heading. Since exchange rates are determined by market forces, they can shift significantly in a short time period.

In FOREX, "exchange rates" refer to the relative value on one currency to another. This means that exchange rates express how much one currency is worth with regard to another. As such, you may find that exchange rates function as a price when conducting trades. Depending on the movement of exchange rates, you can make or lose money.

The majority of the action happens in the spot market. This means that the largest volume of trading happens among currency pairs as they are traded based on current exchange rates. The degree with which trading volume increases or decreases is called "volatility." Volatility refers to the changes in the volume of trading. If the volume of trading doesn't change much, then there is little volatility. However, if there are sudden changes, then this would be considered volatility.

Additionally, volatility refers to the fluctuations in exchange rates themselves. When there is a high degree of volatility, there are significant shifts in exchange rates. Often, these shifts are nothing more than pennies on the dollar. Still, when multiplied by thousands, or even millions of dollars, the pennies suddenly add up. Therefore, it's important for you to keep this in mind.

When you set out to trade on the FOREX market, you will find that your trading platform will display exchange rates as they are being calculated through the act of supply and demand. Supply refers to the amount of one currency available on the market, while demand refers to the number of buyers who wish to purchase it. When there is a balance among these two forces, exchange rates remain relatively stable. When there is a significant shift on one side or another, then exchange rates may suddenly swing up or down.

While violent swings in exchange rates are not unheard of, they are uncommon unless there are forces that compel investors to dump one currency and seek refuge in another. Consider this situation:

Investors are loading up on the currency of country X. This causes supply to be in short order as more and more investors are interested in taking positions in this currency. Then, country X announces they have been hit severely by falling oil prices, causing them to default on their external debt. This causes investors to panic and begin dumping their positions in this currency. Since investors are now looking to find shelter, they begin to dump currency X and buy US Dollars. This causes the relative price of the US Dollar to go up in relation to currency X.

This example might seem a bit extreme, but it has happened throughout history. So, it's not uncommon to see such situations, especially in countries that don't have a stable political situation. As we will discuss later on, it's important for investors to be cognizant of a country's political stability and economic outlook. These are the main factors that can help you determine if you are getting into a safe deal, or you might be opening up yourself to unwanted risk.

Futures Market

The futures market, as the name implies, deals with transactions that will be completed at some point in the future. The futures market is governed by contracts between buyer and seller. In these contracts, the seller agrees to sell at a specific exchange rate while the buyer agrees to purchase at that specific exchange rate.

These contracts are conducted for two main reasons:

The first reason, both buyer and seller are concerned about volatility. As such, they are keen on making sure that they can lock in a given exchange rate so they can avoid having to pay a higher rate or having to sell at a lower one. This is done for purely speculative reasons. Now, it should be noted that not all futures contracts create an obligation to either buyer or seller. In fact, some contracts are called "options." Under the concept of an option, investors can choose not to buy or sell under the specific terms of the contract itself. These provide a great deal of flexibility, especially when volatility is quite high.

The second reason is related to supply. There are times when investors foresee the possibility of shortages in the supply of a currency. So, they might take out a futures contract in order to ensure that they have a guaranteed supply of a specific currency. Later on, these contracts can be sold to other investors who are looking to ensure the supply of a given currency. In such cases, you would not be profiting from the sale of the currency itself. Rather, you would be profiting from the sale of the contract.

Lastly, the futures market is a very important part of FOREX, as it allows investors to protect their positions in the long run. This is a clear difference from the spot market, as the spot market mostly deals with short-term deals. In contrast, the futures market deals with trades that may be conducted months into the future. It all depends on the specific terms of the contract itself.

Forward Market

In the forward market, the transactions that occur are generally the same as the futures market, with the difference that the terms and conditions are customizable to suit the needs of the investors. As such, any number of conditions can be used to trigger the contract. The most common condition is time. The contract would have a specific expiration date in which the trade is executed one the deadline is reached. Also, contracts may include very specific conditions such as exchange rates, volatility, and even the number of trades placed. For instance, a forward contract may stipulate that if the two parties engage in five trades over a two-week period, then the forward contract is executed, thereby causing a sixth trade to happen.

This example highlights how conditions can be set up to meet any number of needs so long as the parties involved agree to them. This offers a great deal of flexibility that cannot be found in the spot market. So, do keep this in mind as you may find yourself in need to engage in custom deals, especially if you can find a willing trade partner.

Factors of Influence in the FOREX Market

The previous example highlights the fact that there are many factors that can influence FOREX markets. As such, it's important for you to do your research before jumping into any sort of trade. Most importantly, you need to be aware of the dangers and risks that come with investing in FOREX without understanding the underlying fundamentals supporting the deal you are making.

That is why we are going to look at technical analysis and fundamental analysis as it pertains to the FOREX market.

Technical Analysis

This is the most common research approach in FOREX. Technical analysis consists in the use of statistical tools and models to analyze the behavior patterns of individual currencies and currency pairs. With technical analysis, you can relatively predict the shifts in exchange rates, particularly if you have a great deal of information to work with. As such, you can construct models that will help you make decisions on what currency pairs to invest in and how you can determine how they will work out.

With technical analysis, you will need to read charts and graphs. These charts will reveal the type of information you need to digest in order to place deals. Such information includes trading volume, exchange rates, and trends.

Speaking of trends, recognizing trends is the single most important aspect of FOREX trading. When you learn to recognize trends, you can determine what a currency's valuation might be at any point in the future. Most importantly, you won't be guessing at what price shifts might occur. In fact, you may find yourself making reasonable assumptions based on the information you have analyzed.

When analyzing trends, you will encounter the term known as a "moving average." A moving average consists of the average exchange rate over a given period of time. For instance, you can calculate the moving average by determining the average exchange rate every hour over the course of two trading days. This will provide you with a glimpse of the currency's behavior.

By the same token, trend can help you determine if it is bullish or bearish. A bullish trend means that that one currency's value is gaining in relation to another. A bearish trend means that one currency's value is diminishing in relation to another.

On the whole, technical analysis is considered to be the cornerstone of FOREX investing. When you are able to harness the power that comes with this kind of information, you will be able to make sound investment decisions every single time.

Fundamental Analysis

The other core element of FOREX market analysis is called "fundamental analysis." Fundamental analysis takes into consideration political, economic, and social factors that might affect a currency's valuation. Please keep in mind that the valuation of a currency depends on a country's overall situation more than what investors perceive to be the value of a currency. In fact, investors will look to the relative stability of a country as an indicator of a currency's value.

This is why the US Dollar, the Euro, and the Swiss Franc are all considered to be "safe" currencies. On the other hand, when you have a country that does not have a stable political situation, you will find that investors will try to avoid putting too many assets into that currency as there is no guarantee where that currency's valuation will head.

Moreover, political factors can literally make, or break, a currency's valuation. Earlier, we highlighted how oil prices can tank a currency's value. Additionally, currency may be propped up by news of strong economic data. This implies that countries that receive positive reviews from economic forecasters may find their currency experiencing an increase in its value as investors will perceive it to be "safer" as opposed to other currencies which may lack greater backing from their country's government or economic outlook.

So, it's best to keep an eye on social, economic, and political news as being aware of these factors can keep your investments safe while avoiding serious losses.

Basic Trading Terms

In this section, we are going to discuss some basic terminology.

- **Cross rate**. This is the value of one currency expressed in another. Commonly, you will find a cross rate to be expressed in the following manner: CHFEUR. In this example, the Swiss Franc (CHF) is expressed in terms of the Euro (EUR). Therefore, when reading the cross rate, you get the value of the Swiss Franc expressed in Euros. So, a cross rate of 1.15 means that for every CHF, you get 1.15 EUR.

- **Exchange Rate**. Exchange rates serve to determine the relative price of one currency in terms of another. Now, you might think that cross rates and exchange rates are the same things. On the surface, they are. The difference lies in that cross rates just compare the value of one currency to another. In fact, you might find that currencies that don't have an exchange rate between them may be to peg their value to a third currency such as the US Dollar. In this case, exchange rates refer specifically to the valuation between two currencies without having to use a third one as a reference. For instance, the exchange rate for the USDEUR pairing may be 0.90. This means that you get 90 cents on the Euro for every US Dollar. Also, cross rates are not necessarily negotiable. However, exchange rates are subject to market forces and can shift at any time.

- **Leverage**. In essence, leverage means that you enter a trade that is greater than the actual amount of money you are investing in. For instance, if you have $100 for a trade, you enter a position that's $1,000. This is a 10 x 1 leverage. If you win, you collect your earnings on $1,000 and not $100. However, if you lose, then you will have to make up the difference of $1,000. In this scenario, you could end up completely wiped out. Novice investors are not cleared to trade using leverage. You need to build up your reputation, so to speak. Also, some trading platforms may ask you to deposit a sum of money as a guarantee that you can cover your margins should you fail to win a trade on leverage. If you trade on leverage and cannot cover the margin, then your positions will be automatically liquidated, and your account may be suspended.

- **PIP**. This is the term used to refer to the "points in percentage" that you can expect to see in the trades you make. Commonly, these points are referred to as "pips." These are relative terms depending on the valuation of the currency. In some cases, a pip may be equal to a penny. In others, it may refer to 1/100th of a penny. It all depends on the relative valuation of one currency with regard to another.

- **Margin**. This refers to the amount of money you need to have deposited in your account. Some platforms require new investors to have a 100% margin. This means that if you deposit $100, you can only trade up to $100. If you have 1%, then you can trade up to $10,000. This means that you don't actually need to have the $10,000 to open a position valued at $10,000. All you need is to have the requisite funds deposited. However, if you should lose out on the deal, you will face a "margin call." In this case, you will have to pony up the cash to cover the margin call. Otherwise, your account may even be canceled.

- **Spread**. This is the difference between the buy and sell quote of a currency pair. The difference is expressed in terms of pips. For instance, is you have a pairing such as AUDCDN expressed as 1.17/04, it means that the upper and lower limits on the deal are 1.1700 - 1.1704. To break even, your deal must make at least 4 pips.

CHAPTER 2

Beginners Guide To Forex Trading

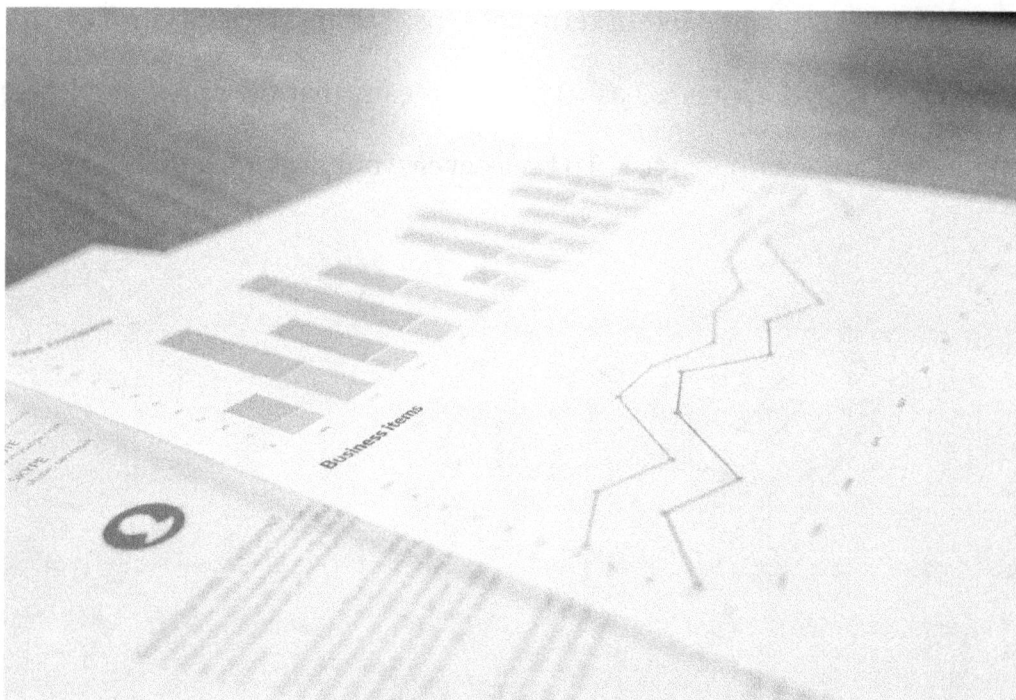

Getting started with FOREX depends greatly on your ability to master the various techniques that come along with it. This means that you need to be at least moderately proficient in computer skills. Having such skills will go a long way toward helping you quickly master FOREX trading, thereby helping you make money right away.

As such, it is important for you to become familiar with the software known as a "trading platform." A trading platform is a piece of software that you use as a means of accessing the FOREX market, therefore, allowing you to trade. You can get started with something as simple as a download. Of course, that is only scratching the surface.

It should be noted that mastering a trading platform requires a combination of study and experience. So, it's always best to make sure you have the right training prior to making your first official trades.

One very important piece of advice is to take advantage of the free demo account that comes with most trading platforms. If you are looking into a platform that does not offer a free demo account, then you might be better off searching for one that does.

The advantage of a free demo account is that you can play with monopoly money as you learn the ways of the platform and FOREX trading in general. You see, demo accounts are intended to give you access to the real market, analytics, and tools, but without actually putting your money at risk. So, you are simply running a simulation of what your real trades would be.

This is a vital part of your training.

By taking advantage of this, you can avoid costly mistakes. Since you are playing with monopoly money, you can make as many mistakes as you need to so that you don't actually lose out when you go live for the real thing.

That being said, we are going to discuss trading platforms and what they imply in this chapter. So, let's take a deep look at what you can expect.

Trading Platforms

Not all trading platforms are created equal.

This means that you need to do your research when it comes to choosing a trading platform. The main differences lie in the analytics and resources that a platform has to offer. You cannot expect a platform to provide you with everything you need if they are not fully transparent in what they have to offer. Moreover, the best platforms are the ones that offer you a demo account. That way, you can test out the platform for yourself before committing to any subscription plans.

In essence, any solid trading platform must offer you two things: access to all the trading tools you need and real-time analytics. These two elements will determine how useful a trading platform is, in addition to giving you the full range of tools you need to conduct successful trades.

It's also important to note that trading platforms should offer you both a desktop and mobile versions. This is key, as you may not always be sitting at your computer. Consequently, having the option to conduct trades, or manage your account, from your mobile device is crucial. This can enable you to move around, especially if you travel frequently.

Trading platforms usually charge you two types of fees. First, trading platforms charge a subscription fee. This could be a one-time setup fee or an annual subscription. Depending on the range of services the platform offers, this is what you can expect to pay. If you have a basic platform service that doesn't offer you real-time analytics and up-to-date information, then you can expect to pay a plat registration fee. On the other hand, if you expect real-time analytics and robust data management, then you may find that you will have to pay an upfront registration fee plus an annual subscription. The fact of the matter is that it's best to pay the additional fee because real-time analytics is worth every penny you can spend.

The second type of fee which you can expect to pay is a fee per trade. Most platforms will charge you pennies per trade. This is something which you must factor into each trade you make as these fees can quickly add up. Therefore, it's worth keeping in mind that finding a platform that doesn't charge you high trade fees is always a good option.

Also, please keep in mind that most trading platforms see bundles. These bundles offer a lot of trades, say, 10 trades for $1.99. These bundles are worth the expense as they can help you to plan your overall cost per trade, thereby allowing you to visualize how much you stand to gain.

How to Use MetaTrader 4

MetaTrader 4 is the most robust trading platform you will find on the market. It has been built to handle all of your FOREX trading needs. It contains everything from the trading platform itself to the robust technical analysis tools you need. This is why MetaTrader 4 is a great choice for your trading needs. Best of all, you don't have any hidden fees or upfront costs. In fact, dealing with MetaTrader 4 is rather straightforward. As such, you don't have to concern yourself with any unpleasant surprises.

MetaTrader 4 actually consists of several components. So, let's take a look at each one:

The MetaTrader 4 Trading Syste

The trading system is the main platform itself. It allows you to place the trades you want to place with virtually any currency pairing available on the market. Its robust capabilities enable you to put any strategy together regardless of how complex it is. This is what makes this trading system the most robust on the market.

It is also a very flexible and convenient option. It provides you with the best tools you need, such as market and pending orders. As such, market orders are the actual buy/sell orders you place as part of your trading strategy. Pending orders are trades that you can set up to be executed later on, for example, at a later date or under specific conditions such as a certain price point or trading volume level. In addition, you have access to trading charts, stop orders (including a trailing stop), a tick chart, and trading history. This is what makes the trading platform so strong yet flexible.

The trading platform allows you to carry out the following types of actions:

- Three different types of execution modes
- Two kinds of market orders
- Four types of pending orders
- Two kinds of stop orders including the use of a trading stop

These tools enable you to get any of your strategies up and running in short order. So, the only thing you need to do is put your strategy together so that the trading platform can execute it for you.

MetaTrader 4 Analytics

What good is a robust trading platform without the right analytics to back it up?

In this case, you get the analytics you need to set up successful trades every time. While the trading system is quite good, the analytics capabilities of MetaTrader 4 are even better. With it, you can access online quotes for up to 9 periods. Also, you can access interactive charts that can enable you to customize the type of information displayed. You can toggle the details so that they can reflect any price changes throughout a given period.

In addition, you will find a total of 23 analytical objects that include 30 built-in indicators that will simplify your trading tasks. This allows you to spend more time thinking about strategy and less time searching for useful information.

The analytics pack also includes the free Code Base app, which allows you to generate thousands of additional indicators. These indicators give you a wide assortment of analytical tools to help you make the most of each trade. The best part is that having a variety of indicators at your disposal enables you to make timely decisions as real-time data comes in.

With the analytics pack you will find:

- A series of interactive charts

- Nine different timeframes which you can analyze
- Twenty-three analytical objects to choose from
- Thirty technical indicators to help you make the most of your research

These are all included when you sign up.

Copy-Trading and Trading Signals

When you are pressed for time, you can simply copy-cat trades. Yes, that's right. With this function, you can copy-cat trades from other successful investors. This is the ultimate way to piggyback on great trades. Of course, you're not stealing anyone's hard work here. What you are doing is implementing a successful strategy. This is important when you don't have the time to sit down and craft your own strategies. This is a great tool, especially when you are on the run.

All you have to do is subscribe to any given signal. These are offered by specific providers. Some of them are free, while others are paid. The best part about using signals is that you can immediately put them to the test in your free demo account. As such, you can see which ones work and which ones don't. You can choose from various levels of risk and return. So, there is something for all tastes. If you want to play it safe, there are safer deals. If you want to run a bit more risk, there's that, too.

With this function, you can expect to find thousands of providers, thousands of trading strategies, and virtually all kinds of trading conditions you can imagine. Indeed, using copy-cat trading, you can quickly learn the ropes of FOREX trading from successful pros. Since there are plenty of free signals, it won't cost you anything extra to give it a try.

Using the MetaTrader Market

This function is quite interesting. It grants you access to an expert advisor. This means that you have access to any number of investment guidelines from real pros. You can purchase access to thousands of these apps, or you can choose free ones. They deliver useful advice which you can put into practice when designing your strategy. In addition, you can use them to customize your trading plans as real-time information flows in.

Also, you can search for the latest technical indicators. This is another great function as it allows you to detect which indicators reflect the best types of analytics you need to stay on top of the latest market trends. The best part of all is that you have a wide selection of both free and paid options. This makes it far easier for you to make sense of your trading needs.

Algorithmic Trading

This is where things get really interesting.

One of the core elements of successful trading is to conduct extensive market research. This is important as you need to be aware of the trends and latest updates on markets. This means that you need to be aware of what's happening.

However, this is not only time-consuming but also very tough to do, especially when you don't have much time. So, this is where algorithmic trading comes into play. Modern trading tools utilize algorithmic trading based on available market information. Then, an algorithm can be developed in order to reflect the trend in markets. The end result is a trading strategy based on the latest information and successful practices.

MetaTrader 4 allows you to integrate both algorithmic trading and Expert Advisor so that you can craft an automatic trading strategy. This implies that you can take much of the research out of trading while crafting a trading strategy that truly reflects the current information available in the marketplace.

This is what folks commonly refer to as "bots." The bots that you are able to create and automate your trades so that all you need to do is push the "trade" button, and the bot takes care of the rest for you. This is ideal for anyone who is looking to invest in FOREX but doesn't have a great deal of time to devote to research and trading.

MetaTrader 4 offers the following applications:

- MQL4 trading strategy editing language
- MetaEditor
- The strategy tester
- A library of free trading bots

Of course, if you are a bit more tech-savvy, you can develop your own trading bots. The neat thing about it is that your own bots can reflect your personal trading strategy.

Mobile Trading

MetaTrader 4 is designed to run on Android and iOS devices. This is the perfect complement to its robust toolkit, especially when you are on the go. For investors who are always on the move, having access to their trading platform on their mobile devices provides a great deal of flexibility. In particular, it allows you to keep up with the latest trends and information. Practically all traders who use MetaTrader 4 have their desktop application along with the mobile app. This is a great way of staying in the loop all the time.

Basic Forex Terminologies

In this section, we are going to look at three crucial terms that you need to become highly familiar with when trading in FOREX.

Price in Points

Price in points, or pips, are essentially the points that you expect to win, or lose, every time you enter a trade. In the previous chapter, we mentioned the function of pips and how you can use them to visualize the amount of money you can make per trade.

In general, pips represent pennies, or fractions of pennies, that you expect to earn on each deal. As such, pips are dependent on the cross rate between two currencies. If the cross rate isn't very large, then a single pip represents a greater degree of value than in a cross rate, which is rather extensive.

By the same token, pips are the standard measure that is used to determine the entry and exit points, as well as the various stop-loss levels in which you can set your trades. As a result, it's important to note that you need to keep the pip calculation in mind all the time.

The great thing about using a trading platform is that the platform does the math for you. As such, all you need to do is focus on the recommended pip points per trade. For instance, there are trading strategies that recommend leaving the trade after earning 20 pips. Don't worry if that doesn't make total sense at this point. The main thing to keep in mind is that your trading platform can take care of this for you. If you choose, you can also do the math yourself. In such cases, it's important to go over the data you are analyzing so that you can be sure that you have the most accurate and up-to-date information.

Lot Sizes

A lot size is the amount of currency you are going to purchase, or sell, in a given trade. The smallest lot size you can purchase in a single deal is one unit of a currency. For instance, you can purchase one US Dollar in exchange for, however, many units of the other currency you need. Additionally, there is no limit to the lot size, meaning that you could purchase millions of units of another currency. Nevertheless, this is not something that is customary as the average investor needs to be wary of their trading capital.

As for large institutional investors, they can really move the price action by purchasing massive lot sizes. These types of investors, for example, hedge funds, make massive deals in which they move millions of Dollars from one currency to the next. It's important to note that these types of investors engage in such trading for the sake of moving their money into markets that offer a greater deal of profit.

For the average investor, a lot size is important as it will determine the overall amount of money that will be invested in a single trade. In general, the golden rule of money management says that you should invest no more than 2% of your total trading capital in a single trade. As a result, you need to make sure that you don't exceed this parameter. Of course, you could invest your entire trading capital at once, but it just wouldn't be in a single deal. That drives up risk too high and could leave you bankrupt should something go wrong.

Limits and Stops

One of the greatest features of modern trading is the existence of limits and stops. Old school investors needed to be cognizant of the price action in such a manner that they could pull the plug on their deals before it was too late. This required investors to be glued to the ticker during the trading day.

Nowadays, this is not necessary. With automated trading, you can set up limits and stops to keep your investments safe. This is why becoming familiar with limits and stops is a must for every FOREX investor.

In essence, limits are used to set a point at which you will sell. Once the limit point is set, a sale order is triggered. The reason for this is that once the limit is reached, it is believed that the price will go down from there. Therefore, you stand to make less profit as compared to selling at the highest point.

Also, limits are used when looking to purchase. As such, limits are triggered when the price reaches a certain point. When that point is reached, the investor enters the trade. If the price point is not triggered, then the trade does not happen. That is why limits are very useful when it comes to setting up a trade based on the expectations that you want.

Stops are used to reduce the number of losses you are willing to accept. These points are also known as "stop-loss." They are quite handy when setting up your trades. A golden rule of FOREX investing is that you must always set up stops. The reason for this is that when a trade suddenly goes bad, you have a point at which you will exit the trade. This means that you cannot expect to continue in the trade at this point. Automated trading platforms have a function that is triggered by a "double stop." When you hit two consecutive stop-loss points, the system can be configured to automatically liquidate any open positions you may have. This type of configuration can save your portfolio from disaster.

CHAPTER 3

Setting Up Your Trading Platform

At this point, we are ready to get started setting up our trading platform. On the whole, MetaTrader 4 makes it very easy for you to get started trading. While you do need a fairly thorough run-through of the trading system, it's quite easy to get things rolling. This is why this chapter is focused on helping you get off the ground quickly and easily.

To get started with MetaTrader 4, you need to download the main software platform from the MetaTrader 4 website. This will download the installer pack, which then runs the platform on your Windows or Mac OS computer. Also, you can install MetaTrader 4 on Linux devices. As such, this gives you the flexibility to run this platform on any device you use. In addition, you can install it on Android and iOS devices.

The platform is available at https://www.metatrader4.com/en/download. So, do take the time to go over the system requirements to make sure that your device is fully equipped to run the platform. The last thing you want is to have your system crash because it doesn't meet the full range of specifications.

Once you have downloaded the MetaTrader 4 platform, you will be instructed to create an account. Simply enter your email address, and you'll be good to go. Also, you'll need to enter some personal information. This is standard stuff. At this point, you'll be prompted to choose between the full account and the free demo account.

Here is one of the most crucial investment decisions you'll ever make: choose the free demo account! You'll be granted access for 15 days. Do not forego the option to choose the free demo account as that would lead you to the full paid account. If you do this, you'll be trading directly with your own funds. In that case, you'll have to be very careful as mistakes can quickly add up and torch your investment capital. This is why the demo account is the best way to get started.

Later on, you can migrate into the full account. At that point, you'll have to provide a source of funds (a bank account or credit card) in addition to the various information items you'll be requested to fill out (mainly government regulation stuff).

Once you are on board with the free demo account, you'll have access to the full functionality of MetaTrader 4. Since there are no restrictions, you can get a great sense of what the platform has to offer. So, make wise use of your time. You can browse everything available to paid users. The only difference is that the winnings you make won't actually count. By the same token, if you miss out on some deals, it won't affect your account. In fact, if you get wiped out, the system will refresh your investment capital. However, there is a limited amount of times you can do this (two times). So, if you get wiped out twice, you won't be able to trade again until you actually top up your account with real funds.

One other thing: do take the time to go over the various types of views and displays. In doing so, you can set up the trading system so that it reflects your personal preferences and the setup you feel most comfortable with. Since you'll most likely be dealing with a great deal of charts and information, it's best to have a setup that you would feel most comfortable with. While some investors like to have a two or three-screen setup, MetaTrader 4 is designed to run on a single screen. However, feel free to customize it to suit your individual needs.

How to Use Trading View

Once you have MetaTrader 4 up and running on your computer, all you need to do is use ctrl+T to open and close the main window. Of course, you'll need to make sure that the platform is running. If you log out and end the session on your computer, you won't be able to use this shortcut. So, do make sure that the platform is currently running. The default configuration sets MetaTrader 4 to run on startup. So, it'll be loaded every time you turn on your computer unless you choose to do otherwise.

When you open up MetaTrader 4, you'll be set into "trading view." This is the default view for the platform. That way, all you need to do is open up the platform and begin trading. You'll have access to all trading features at this point.

Trade History

The "trade history" feature enables you to see the trades you have placed throughout your time on the platform. To access your trade history, all you need to do is click on the "Account History" tab. This tab is located across the top of the main window. Alternatively, you can right-click anywhere on the screen to reveal the drop menu. Once open, you can select the "All History" function. This feature allows you to visualize your entire trading history for the "last month" or the "last 3 months". Clicking on any of these options will display your history on the screen. You can also select to save your history data by clicking on "Detailed Report." This option allows you to generate a detailed report for your trading activity.

The great thing about this reporting feature is that it allows you to get information on the various aspects pertaining to your trades. Here, you view the price, lot size, execution time, profit, loss, and the date and time. This is highly useful as this allows you to review successful trades while also going over unsuccessful ones.

When you choose the "Save as Report" or "Save as Detailed Report" function, you'll be displayed this information on a new tab in your web browser. To save this information on your computer, click on any part of the screen on the hit ctrl+A to select all. Once the text is highlighted, all you need to do is copy and then paste on any word processing program such as Microsoft Word. You can then save the file directly on to your computer. This will also allow you to print a hard copy if you wish.

If you wish to display your trade history in chart form, you need to go to the "Account History" tab. Then, choose any trade by clicking on it and then drag it into a chart window. You will then see the trade displayed as a chart with the open and close levels marked in the chart by arrows. These two points will be joined by a dotted line to reveal the path of the trade. After, simply drag your mouse cursor over the line to see the information pertaining to those points in the trade.

Open Trades

To view open trades, simply open up the terminal. You can either click on the icon in the taskbar or hit ctrl+T. You can then view all open trades by hitting the "trade" tab across the top. All open trades are organized within the same window, so it allows you to visualize the action happening all at once.

Account Balance

To check your account balance, once again open up the terminal. Then, go to the "Trade" tab. There you will find a line that indicates your balance, equity, and free margin. At first, you won't have access to margin beyond a 1:1 ratio. As you gain more traction, the margin will increase. Also, you can request for greater margin.

Trade Level Colors

The default setting for colors for open trades on MetaTrader 4 is green for entry level and red for stop-loss and limit level. In essence, the green dotted line that represents the entry point of the deal is used to help you determine the exact point where you entered the trade. The red dotted line serves to indicate the exit point of the deal. This is also the take-profit point meaning that this is the point in which you would leave the trade successfully.

If you wish to change these colors to others which suit your preferences better, you can do this by going to the "Properties" tab or hitting F8. This will open up the menu in which you can customize these colors. You can choose from any of the colors available. In addition, you can also turn off these colors by going to the "Tools" menu at the top of the menu bar and then in "options" you can uncheck the box for "show" trade levels. This will leave you with a clean looking chart.

However, it is not recommended to turn off trade levels, especially when reviewing past trades, as this will help you to visualize the data in a much friendly manner. In the end, you can choose to customize colors to suit your vision.

Chart Background

All charts have backgrounds on which you can visualize the data. Most traders prefer going with a plain white background, as this gives you the easiest means of visualizing the data itself. However, you are free to customize this to suit your preferences. To do this, go to the "properties" tab or hit F8. Then, select the "colors" tab just as you did for the trade levels. You will find that the first item is "background color." You can choose any color from the drop-down menu. It's always a good idea to try out various colors so that you can decide which colors work best for you.

Working With Indicators

MetaTrader 4 is loaded with indicators. It comes pre-loaded with over 50 various indicators. These core indicators are set up automatically when you install MetaTrader 4 for the first time. For the most part, you might not see the need for additional indicators. The core indicators may be more than enough to meet your trading needs.

However, you might find that as you come up with more complex strategies, you'll need to work with an expanded set of customized indicators. This is important as your particular trading strategies may require you to search for more specific information. Therefore, you'll also need to make use of customized indicators.

So, we're going to be looking at how indicators work in MetaTrader 4.

On the whole, indicators are technical analysis tools that you can use to determine trends that you can use to support your models and strategies. These indicators can be used to provide you with reasonable assumptions about future price movements.

With MetaTrader 4, you get a number of indicators that are free. Then, you have a number of additional add-ons that are either free or paid, depending on the source. When you sign up for your demo account, be sure to check out which indicators are freely available to you. That way, you can play with them to see how they can help you make your assumptions.

Let's take a look at some of the indicators which you can use to help you visualize your trading activity.

Order History Indicator

With this indicator, you can go over any past trades while overlaying them onto any chart. This will enable you to recreate past trades using existing data so that you can determine if you are setting yourself up for success. Likewise, you can copy and paste other investors' trades and overlay them on any chart. This will enable you to see how the deal might play out.

Pivot Points Indicator

With this indicator, you can determine where pivot points may be located. For instance, you can set up a given pivot point based on previous market activity. This will enable you to determine where you might see potential changes in trend. Additionally, these pivot points can help you figure out if you are lining up a trade correctly. You can also set up alerts so that you are notified when a given point you have set up has been hit.

Hight and Low Indicator

This tool allows you to look up high and low points for any pairing on any chart in any given time period. This is great for when you are mulling over previous data. It enables you to determine when specific points were located within previous time periods. With the highs and lows, you can determine if your assumptions are correct or if you need to make any adjustments based on the historical data.

Trend Lines

These are, by far, the most popular indicators on any FOREX platform. Trend analysis is a fundamental tool of technical analysis. This indicator will allow you to visualize where the trends are moving for a given currency pairing. As a result, you can either play a trend -following strategy, or you can devise a countertrend strategy. The main idea here is to visualize both the trend line and the candlesticks for each period. Candlesticks are vertical bars that measure the open, close, and average prices during a given period. You can adjust these candlesticks to reflect hourly data, for example, or if you are looking at longer timeframes, you can look at daily data.

Chart Grouping

When you are working on multiple charts, this indicator works perfectly. What it allows you to do is to make changes simultaneously on various charts. This works really well when you are testing out a strategy across various time periods or with different currency pairs. You can group various charts regardless of the data contained. As such, it provides you with the robust capabilities you need to make the best of the data you have on hand.

Freehand Drawing

If you need to make customized notations, symbols, and other marks on any chart, you can select the freehand editor. This allows you to draw directly on the chart. You can draw your own trend lines, entry, and exit points, while also using various colors to highlight the information you are looking to make visible. Best of all, you don't need to have any special drawing tools. The indicator app allows you to do it directly on the chart.

Add-on Indicators

There are hundreds of indicators that you can add on to your platform. Feel free to browse through the free selections as they are ready for integration. However, the paid ones would require you to test them out first before committing to purchasing them. Among add-ons, you'll find stealth others, correlation calculators, task and alarm managers while also PIP calculators, and much more. Some of these add-ons are developed by some companies in order to promote their services, while others have been developed by fellow users who share them with all FOREX traders.

When you are working with the free demo account, make sure you give all free indicators the proper due diligence. That way, you know which ones you can incorporate into your trading strategy once you live. As for the paid ones, it's probably best to take advantage of any free trials before committing to your purchase. While they will do no harm to your portfolio, you might end up spending cash on tools you won't be using. So, it's always a good idea to test things out first before committing to a purchase.

Installing Add-ons

In addition to the pre-loaded indicators (which you can find by selecting the "navigator" window and then the "indicators" folder), you can install any of the indicators available to you. While you can search around for available indicators, your best bet at gaining access to virtually every indicator is through the MetaTrader Supreme Edition. This is a plug-in that is installed on the MetaTrader 4 platform. This plug-in comes in loaded with a host of indicators that plug right into your terminal. As such, you won't have to look around for them. This bundle offers a great combination of tools without having to break the bank. You can download it for free to test. After the trial version expires, you can choose to go for any of the pricing packs available.

Now, if you choose to install an add-on yourself, go to the "navigator" tab and go to "indicators." There you can choose the "browse" option to search the various types of indicators that are available for download. When you choose the one you like, you need to search for the MT4 data file. This file will be in your "downloads" folder. Now, select it and paste it to your clipboard. Once you are ready, go to the "file" tab and choose "Open Data Folder." This will open the "MQL4" folder, which then leads you to the "indicators" folder. Here, you can paste the downloaded file you copied to your clipboard. And, that's all there is to it! The new indicator should now appear when you open the "indicators" section of the "Navigator" tab.

Turning Off an Indicator

Once you have loaded your selected indicators, they will be active at the same time. This can make it easy to follow all of the action that you are looking to keep track of. However, there might be a case in which you don't want to have an indicator working for you anymore. In this case, to turn it off, use the crtl+I shortcut. From there, you'll be displayed a list of indicators. Then, you can select the indicator you wish to turn off. After, click on the "delete" button to make it go away. While this does not permanently delete the indicator, you will have to manually restart it if you wish to have function again. Nevertheless, it's a great tool to have in case you want to simplify things on your terminal.

Analyzing the Market

Being a successful FOREX investor requires a good dose of due diligence. This means analyzing the information that's available on the market. In a manner of speaking, it's like sports teams watching game film of themselves and their opponents. In doing so, they can be ready to attack the opposition when they take the field. Most importantly, it enables the team to develop a strategy that they can put to use when going on the field.

As such, market analysis is critical in the FOREX market. You cannot expect to be successful by simply placing trades haphazardly. You need to have analytics that can enable you to make the right investment decisions, given your expectations and risk tolerance.

The good news is that MetaTrader 4 provides you with a great deal of tools to conduct technical analysis. As such, you won't have to scour the internet looking for sources of credible information. However, it's what you do once you get that information that makes the difference between underwhelming returns and actually making money on deals.

So, let's take a look at three important elements of market analysis you need to become familiar with in order to become a truly successful FOREX investor.

Trends

Trend analysis is at the core of technical analysis in all financial markets. As for FOREX, it's vital that you become familiar with trend analysis as this will enable you to get a handle on where the various types of currency pairing may be going.

At a glance, you can quickly spot trends just by looking at a chart. However, the secret to truly analyzing a trend in charts is to spot the potential reversals in that chart. This requires a bit more of a trained eye as not all folks are able to easily spot these points.

Firstly, a bullish trend means that the valuation of one currency is going up with regard to another. When you look at a chart, you can quickly spot a bullish trend by noticing how the line curves upward, then rounds off at the top before beginning to descend. In some cases, you'll find charts moving up and then have a sharp decline in an inverted "V" shape. The goal, in this case, is to follow the trend so that you can get in before the price goes up and capitalize on the highest possible point at which you can exit the trade.

Secondly, a bearish trend is the opposite of a bullish trend. You can quickly spot a bearish trend by seeing the line dip down to the bottom of the chart in a "U" shape. If the recovery in price is quick, it will resemble a "V" shape. In either case, you'll find that getting out of a trade before the line hits the bottom is essential to either minimizing losses, or perhaps finding a potential entry point.

Lastly, when the line trades at a seemingly horizontal manner, then you are looking at a "sideways" trend. In this case, you are seeing how the currency pair is trading in a "band." The term "band" means that the pairing is in a tight range in such a way that there isn't much room to maneuver. When this occurs, it's either due to low trading volume or perhaps investors looking to get in at a specific point in time.

With MetaTrader 4, charts automatically calculate trends both in real-time and with historical data. This makes it a valuable tool when looking to make the most of the data you have available. If you are looking to trade with the trend, then it is quite easy to just follow the charts. If you are looking to follow a countertrend strategy, then you really need to pay close attention to any signs of a potential reversal.

Ranges

It is quite common for certain currency pairs to trade in a specific range or "band." In these cases, you have predictable movements in price. These movements are usually the reflection of investor sentiment when it comes to price action in that pair. Additionally, it is quite common to find that correlated pairs trade in a band. By "correlated pairs," we're talking about currency pairs that have a long history together. These are currencies that are commonly traded together. As such, there is a plethora of information on these pairings.

Consequently, investors know what to expect. Hence, they build strategies to capitalize on the range they trade in. Unless there is a considerable disruption in the market, you won't find correlated pairs suffering from any unexpected jolts.

Using the technical analysis tools in MetaTrader 4, you can determine these ranges as the charting application will show you the highs and lows. Over time, you can ascertain where these highs and lows can be found. Since currency pairs that trade in a range have a rather predictable fluctuation in their valuation, you can reasonably determine when to get in and when to get out. By following this dynamic, you'll most likely make money practically every time.

Significant Levels

In FOREX, significant levels are those which are charted based on the fluctuations in the pricing of a given currency pair. These levels generally indicate a reversal in trend. For instance, if a currency pairing is trading with a bullish trend, this trend will eventually hit a significant level at which investors are signaled to get out of the trade unless they risk losing money. When you set up alerts for these levels, they will quickly flash on the screen. This is where you can exit the trade manually or set up a limit in order to automatically liquidate your position when you hit that mark.

By the same token, if a currency pair is trading on a bearish trend, the significant level may be triggered to indicate that there is a potential reversal coming. When this occurs, the reversal may signal that it's time to get in. In such cases, you can capitalize on the upswing.

It should be noted that significant levels are also based on trading volume. When trading volume picks up, the system notices this. It then takes into account where the trendline would be moving based on the increased activity. This is important when considering that increased trading volume may be a signal that it's time to get out. If you happen to spot a high trading volume on the "sell" side, then it might be time for you to get out. In contrast, if you detect that a large number of investors are taking positions in a given trend, then it might be a good time to ride the wave.

So, do make sure that you set up alerts to notify you of changes in significant levels. This will help you spare yourself from complicated situations down the road.

CHAPTER 4

Taking Action In The Market

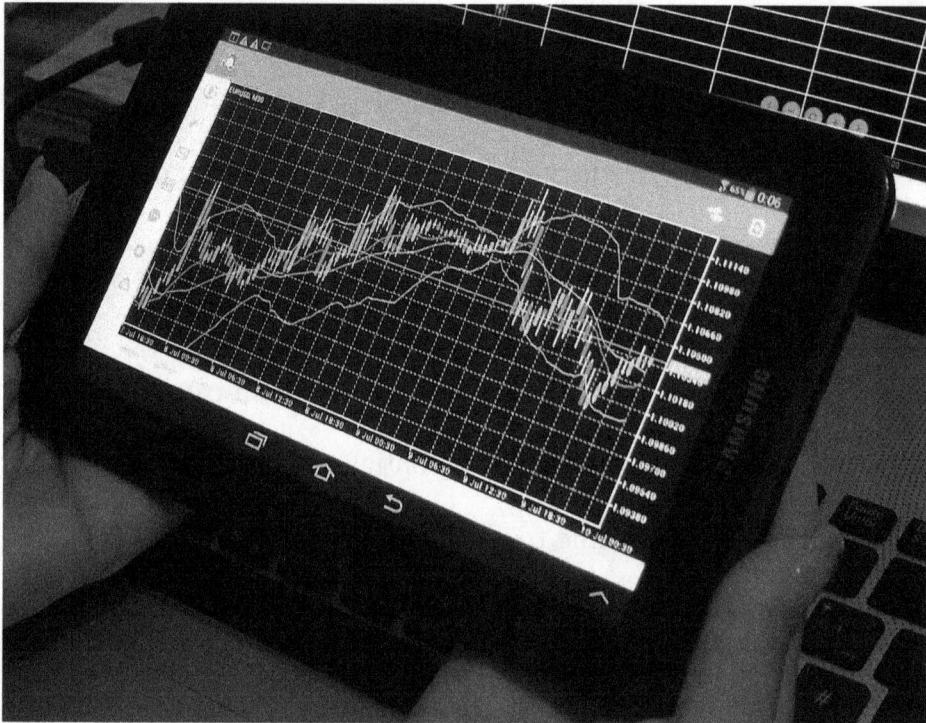

Now that we have covered the basics of the trading system and how you can begin to capitalize on FOREX trades, the time has come to begin getting our hands dirty. In this chapter, we are going to be taking a look at how you can begin to take action in the market. As such, you can begin to craft your initial strategies just as you would once you go live.

As a FOREX investor, it's important for you to understand the way that price is set in the market. As mentioned earlier, the currency market is ruled by the forces of supply and demand. This means that buyers come to the market along with sellers in hopes of swapping what each other is looking to get.

In a traditional market, buyers come loaded with money in order to purchase items that they need. In the case of sellers, they take their wares to the marketplace in hopes of obtaining money in exchange. In FOREX, you are essentially trading money for money. It may seem somewhat counterintuitive, but that's what you are essentially doing.

This is a clear difference from the stock market in which you are exchange money for shares of a company. Nevertheless, the FOREX market is highly liquid, meaning that there is an abundance of cash all the time. Therefore, you can reasonably liquidate your position any time you need money.

This isn't something which you can easily do with the stock market.

FOREX investors are keenly aware of all the various elements that influence the valuation of currency. In the section on fundamental analysis, we discussed how important political, social, and economic events are in the overall valuation of a currency. There is no question that all of these elements play a key role.

However, all of these elements need to come together at some point. That point is price. Price is the reflection of all the factors that determine the valuation of currencies in the market. Whether these elements are fundamental in nature, or whether they are technical, these elements all come together to produce an effect in price. In this case, price refers to the cross rates between two currencies.

So, this chapter is going to take a look at price action and how you can use this approach to help you define your initial trading strategy.

Using Price Action Strategy

In FOREX, "Price Action" refers to a discipline that helps you to determine how to conduct trades. While there are several tools such as moving averages that help to determine support and resistance levels, the fact of the matter is that price is the sole indicator that reflects any changes that may be taking place in the market. This is important to consider when analyzing both fundamental and technical data.

To capitalize on Price Action strategy, you need to analyze the trend in prices over a given period of time. This can be done with charts generated by your trading platform. These charts chart price movements based on the statistical tool called a "candlestick." Earlier, we mentioned that candlesticks are used to measure the open and close prices of a pair in addition to the average. This is important to keep in mind as longer candlesticks indicate a greater divergence between the open and close prices, while a shorter one indicates a narrower difference.

You will find the there are several indicators that are used to determine FOREX strategy. These include the MACD (moving average convergence divergence strategy), the RSI (Relative Strength Index) or the Stochastic Oscillator. These measurements look to model the movements in price. However, they are often inaccurate as they don't take the whole picture of what's happening in the price.

Perhaps the best indicator aside from price itself is the moving average as it charts the average price of a currency pair over a given period of time. The end result is a chart that plots the average price over a time period, thereby revealing the trend of the price of two currencies.

The RSI and Stochastic Oscillator are based on trading volume. Taking these measures into account as your main trading information can be deceitful as there could be any number of reasons for the increased trading volume. Therefore, the only true, accurate measure of movement is price.

The Basics of Price Action

To use Price Action strategy as part of your overall trading strategy, it's important for you to become familiar with price charts. As we've mentioned, your platform can generate these for you using any timeframe you choose.

To get started with Price Action, here are some ground rules to keep in mind:

1. When you begin testing out a strategy, it's best to stick to it for as long as you can. Often, investors make the mistake of hopping from one strategy to another. For instance, if you choose to use the MACD, then stick to it until you master it. This will enable you to get a sense of where this strategy will take you, particularly when considering the complexity of the elements involved. You will find that successful investors start out by mastering

one strategy. Once they see that it can provide them with good returns, they can move on to try out others. If it doesn't meet their expectations, they can try another.

2. Also, focus on higher timeframes when analyzing data. A timeframe can be a month, a week, or even a day. By the same token, you can analyze years of data. In this case, it's always best to analyze higher timeframes. For instance, you can look at the action over a month or more. This helps to eliminate any unjustified spikes in trading, which may convince you of unreasonable trading. This is important to note as sudden events may impact investor psyche, therefore, leading to a spike in trading. This is important to bear in mind as overtrading can catch up to you. By "overtrading," we mean placing too many trades in a short period of time. You might get sucked into this trap if you look at lower timeframes such as a week or just a couple of days.

3. Perhaps the easiest way to begin mastering Price Action is to copy successful trades. This might seem like a no-brainer, but it actually makes a lot of sense. When you copy successful trades, you can gain a sense of how to determine what to do in any given situation. As you gain experience, you will be able to set up your own strategy.

When starting out with Price Action, take a look at daily charts. Daily charts are a great way of spotting patterns. For example, you might find that certain currency pairs have a higher trading volume at certain times of the day. This may be the reflection of other markets opening and closing. Also, you may notice that certain price points trigger buying and selling. Thus, you can figure out where to get in based on these points.

So, let's take a look at some Price Action strategies which will help you get the most out of your trades.

Broken Trendline Retest Strategy

This strategy consists of assuming the behavior of a price will revert to the mean once the mean has been broken. This strategy plays off the fact that all prices eventually revert to their mean unless there are significant changes that can alter their mean. However, alterations in mean usually take a long time (relatively speaking) and do not happen overnight.

In this Price Action strategy, you need to plot a trendline for any currency pair. Generally speaking, the trendline should look into at least 20 time periods (usually a higher timeframe such as an hourly chart). So, you can take a look at the movements over the last 24 to 48 hours. This should provide you with enough information with regard to the overall behavior of the price itself.

Then, you can look for points at which the actual level of the price of the currency pairing breaks trend meaning it trades above or below the actual trendline. When this occurs, you can assume the price will return back to its original trend. This is where you can bank on profits being made. In addition, you can predict with reasonable certainty that the price will eventually shift back to where you originally spotted it.

To double check your strategy, you can go back to look at similar periods in which the valuation of the currency pairing broke the trendline. In such cases, you must study to see how long it took for the currency pairing to return to trend. In some instances, it might be a question of a few hours. In other instances, it might even take days. At the end of the day, it largely depends on the prevailing market conditions. Nevertheless, previous behavior should give you a very clear indication of what to expect.

You don't need any special indicators for this strategy to work. In fact, all you need is a price chart that contains at least hourly information. However, it is not recommended that you look at lower timeframes, such as daily data, as you could miss a great deal of information. So, a good rule of thumb is to take an hourly chart that goes back roughly 24 to 48 hours.

Resistance and Support Levels

To make the break and retest strategy functional, you need to focus on the support and resistance levels, as seen in price trends. Essentially, a support level is the lowest level that the price will touch down before rebounding back up. On the other hand, a resistance level is the highest point at which a price will hit before coming back down.

When looking at these levels, you can ascertain the band in which a currency pair is trading. Consequently, you can determine how low a price will go and how high it will reach. Generally speaking, you can determine these points by looking at the price action for the last 24 to 48 hours.

A good rule of thumb is to observe resistance and support levels, hitting at least three consecutive times. When you see this (the actual figure of a support or resistance level is always the exact same though it's very close), you can assume that any divergence of these support levels will mean a reversion to mean.

Let's assume that you are tracking the USDEUR pairing. You observe a support level of 1 and a resistance level of 1.05. This implies that the pairing will be trading in this range. During the period you are observing, you notice that the low point has hit 1, or at least very close to it. Once this point is hit, the price bounces back up to a max of 1.05. At that point, the price will come back all the way down to 1 and back up. When you notice this action for at least 3 times, you can assume that any time the price breaks through any of these points, you can assume a reversion back to mean.

So, here is where you can implement the strategy: track the price movement over a given period. When you see the price touch down to the support or hit the resistance level, then you need to be on the lookout for the price breaking either level. You can set up your trade so that it goes through as soon as the price breaks either point. Your entry point can be above or below the break while your exit point can be once the price reverts to mean.

A word of caution: be careful using this strategy when there is a high degree of volatility, as seen in wild swings in price or trading volume. In these cases, you may have unusual price action, which may take longer than expected to revert to mean.

Engulfing Bar Candlestick Pattern

In this strategy, we are going to be looking at the use of candlesticks as a means of determining price action and potentially identifying reversals. This strategy is highly useful when you are looking to track entry and exit points. Generally speaking, you are tracking price action over a given period of time in such a way that you are looking to determine where the price of a currency pairing will change trend.

There are two types of patterns, a bullish and bearish trend.

The bullish trend refers to price action that is going up. Therefore, you can expect the reversal to indicate a trend back downward. On the whole, you are looking to track the trendline as it hits the highest point of the resistance level. When this happens, the trend would be expected to revert down to mean.

The bearish trend refers to price action that is going down. As such, you expect the reversal to indicate price action moving back up. In general terms, you are looking to identify the exact point in which the trendline hits the lowest point of the resistance level and then changes course.

In both of these approaches, the candlesticks track the trendline indicate when the actual reversal has taken place.

To identify this exact point, track the trendline down to the lowest or highest point. You will notice a very short candlestick. The reversal official occurs when the next candlestick is much larger than the previous one. Thus, the next candlestick "engulfs," that is, it completely covers the previous one.

Let's assume a bearish pattern. In this case, you have the trendline moving downward. If you have been tracking the price action for any length of time, you may have an expectation of where the support level would be. As you observe the trendline moving toward the support level, you will find that the candlesticks are progressively getting shorter and shorter. Then, you will find a very short candlestick followed by a large one immediately following it. This is the reversal. This is the engulfing candlestick. This could serve as an entry point for a trade.

Now, let's assume a bullish pattern. In this situation, you are tracking the highest point in the trend. Thus, you are essentially looking to track an exit point. As the trendline approaches its highest point, that is the resistance level. You will notice every candlestick getting shorter and shorter. Eventually, the shortest candlestick will be followed immediately after by a much longer candlestick that engulfs the previous one. This is the official mark of reversal and should be your exit point. Ideally, you should exit the trade at the point of the shortest candlestick. This is the highest possible point you could achieve before your profit begins to dwindle. Of course, it's virtually impossible to track the exact point of reversal, but anything close to that point would serve well to maximize your profits.

Please note that most trading platforms use red-colored candlesticks to indicate a bearish pattern, while green-colored ones are used to mark a bullish trend. This color-coded system is very useful in helping you figure out how to spot reversals in trend.

Risk Management With Price Action

Risk management is an integral part of any kind of investing. When you follow tried and true risk management practices, you are able to hedge yourself from making mistakes that could wipe out your investment capital.

So, let's take a look at some risk management guidelines which you can implement when you are using Price Action as your main FOREX investment strategy.

1. **Beware of volatility**

   Volatility is the biggest enemy of the Price Action strategy. When you are using Price Action as your main investment strategy, it's important to keep in mind a high degree of volatility can lead to unusual shifts in Price Action. Since prices always tend to revert to mean, you can reasonably assume this will happen eventually. However, when there is a high degree of volatility, prices may return to mean faster or longer than anticipated. As a result, you need to keep your eye on this indicator even though it is not necessary to do so.

2. **Watch for false signals**

   There are times when you get false signals of reversals. For instance, you may get an engulfing candlestick well before the trendline hits the expected resistance or support level. While this is entirely possible, beware as it could simply be the result of unusual trading volume. If you spot a possible reversal well before expected levels, watch out for confirmation. Investors who jump in at the first sign may be in for an unexpected result.

3. Always seek confirmation

On the subject of false signals, always make sure that you get confirmation. If you see a potential reversal that does not fit the usual trading patterns, then it would be best to wait for a confirmation. Confirmation is needed to determine if there might be a new support or resistance level. Three consecutive hits can serve to confirm a new level. Some investors wait for only two hits before assuming there will be a third hit. If you are more risk-tolerant, you can go on two hits before assuming the third hit.

4. Be careful with countertrend investing

When you are starting out, it's best to avoid countertrend investing. The main drawback of this approach is that you anticipate reversals at points in which there may be no technical information to support this assumption. You can go on a hunch, or perhaps as a result of spotting engulfing candlesticks. Still, this is a risky type of investment that you must study carefully.

5. Avoid analyzing lower timeframes

When you are analyzing timeframes, always take higher timeframes. Most FOREX analysts recommend looking at periods of at least one hour. However, this would be too high. Ideally, looking at 20 periods, that is at least 20 hours, is the best way of tracking your strategy. In this book, we recommend looking at charts from 24 to 48 hours so that you can get ample confirmation of your strategy. On the whole, 24 hours is a good timeframe. However, 48 hours will allow you to filter out any price action derived from unusual trading activity.

CHAPTER 5

Price Action Confluence

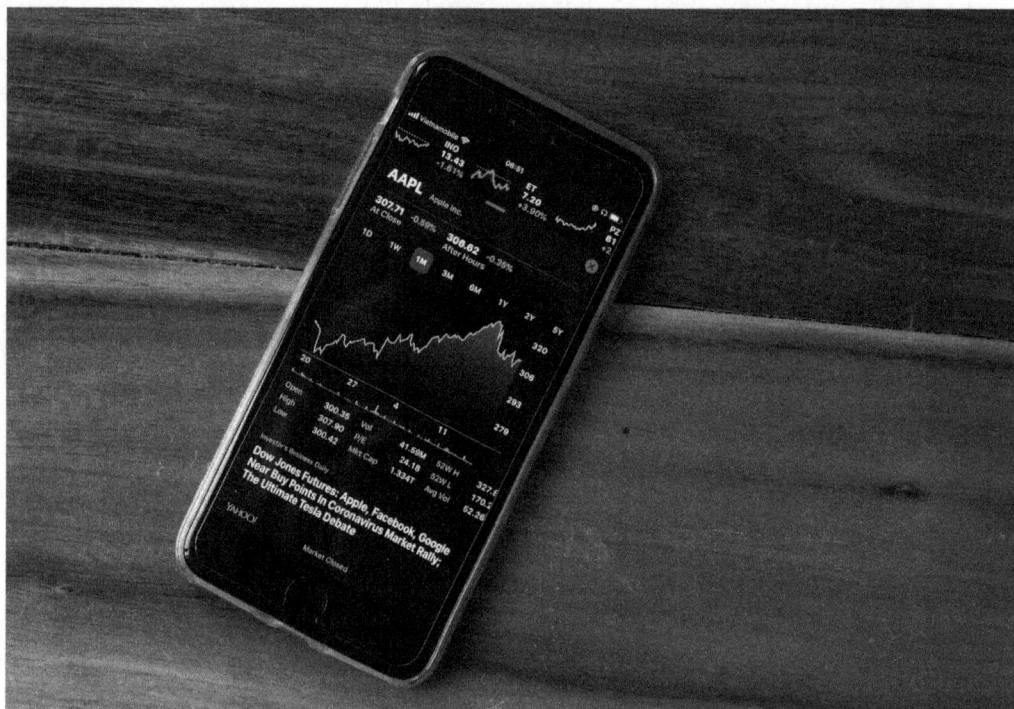

When making use of Price Action as your main trading strategy, you can use confluence to devise your personal investment strategy. In the previous chapter, we discussed how you can use Price Action to determine entry and exit points for your trading strategy. In this chapter, we are going to look at how you can use confluence to set up your trading strategy.

As with all Price Action trades, it's important to keep a close eye on trends. Given the fact that Price Action is dependent on tracking price movements, setting up trades using confluence requires close study of price movements.

On the whole, confluence can be defined as the interaction between two or more levels. This interaction occurs within a single currency pair. As such, you need to be looking at the various levels of price action. For the purpose of this book, we are going to be looking at three specific levels: support, resistance, and trend. These three levels are what you need to track in order to determine confluence.

It is the interaction among the various levels, which makes the strategy work. When you identify the confluence of levels, you can determine entry and exit points, or perhaps spot signals for breakouts.

About Resistance and Support Levels

The simplest way to spot support and resistance levels is by spotting highs and lows. This is the easiest way to identify such levels without resorting to technical analysis tools. If you choose to employ technical analysis tools to determine support and resistance levels, you can get reasonable assurance that these are proven to be accurate. The way in which the platform calculates these levels is by comparing trend to the highs and lows of the timeframe under examination.

Just as we have discussed in earlier sections of this book, you can spot your levels by marking three consecutive hits on the levels you have identified. These consecutive hits must fall within the range. If there are breakouts or breakthroughs, then you need to be reasonably sure that they are within the range you are tracking. Be wary of points that break out of a resistance level as this could signal a new resistance level. By the same token, you need to be wary of price action breaking through a floor as this could signal a new floor. If you fail to spot this possibility, you could enter or exit at the wrong point.

An easy way to spot a new floor or ceiling is through the use of a "double top" or "double bottom." A double top consists of two consecutive hits above the resistance level you have identified. This is observed when there is a bullish trendline. So, you have identified three consecutive hits that you used to establish a ceiling. Then, you detect a hit above the resistance level, which then reverts to the mean. If the next hit pops above the resistance level, then you have just seen a double top. At this point, you can expect a breakout. When the breakout occurs, the third hit will rise above the ceiling. Therefore, you can reasonably assume that the new ceiling is now in place.

On the flip side, price action that breaks through the floor on two consecutive hits is considered as a double bottom. This is seen in a bearish trend. As such, the new floor is established when the trendline hits below the floor two consecutive hits. You can then reasonably assume that the third hit will fall below the floor. This could mark a great entry point if you are looking to play off the rebound.

During this analysis, confluence occurs when the overall trendline intersects the resistance and support levels you have identified. As such, the trendline will ultimately determine what you can expect moving forward.

Understanding the trend

To simplify things, use the charting function in your platform to calculate the trend line. Then, use the information reflected in the chart itself to determine the support and resistance levels. In particular, pay attention to the engulfing candlesticks to signal the reversal in trend as the currency pair trades within its range.

At this point, it's important to keep in mind that even though you have see-sawing action in the price movement, the trend line will ultimately determine if it is a bullish or bearish trend. As always, it's important to analyze charts that contain 24 to 48 hours' worth of data. Nevertheless, you can look at longer timeframes for the sake of spotting similar patterns.

Some investors like to take a look at a weeks' worth of data in order to establish recurring patterns. In such cases, it could be that the specific time window you are looking at does not reflect the trend in the market. While this is rather uncommon, it is possible that you are looking at a period that highlights unusual trading activity.

It should also be noted that trend is very short-term in the case of FOREX. Unlike stocks, FOREX investors live in the present, so to speak. Stock investors look at 20-day, 50-day, and 200-day moving averages. These are clear indicators of where the valuation of a stock may move. In the world of FOREX, things can turn on a dime, especially in times of uncertainty. As a result, you need to focus on the most up-to-date information.

Nevertheless, trend is clearly visible over longer time periods. So, it's worth analyzing longer timeframes for the sake of confirming your assumptions. Additionally, if there are relevant events going on in the world around you, it might be worth taking a closer look at trends well beyond the 48-hour period. It could be that price action was trending in one direction but suddenly reversed as a result of unforeseen events. In this case, think of events such as terrorist attacks, large company bankruptcies, or major political events.

Trendline Confluence

When trendline confluence occurs, you could be setting yourself up for an explosive gain (a breakout), or you could be heading down for a sharp decline (a breakthrough). Thus, understanding the points in which you anticipate confluence may set you up for success or save you from getting hammered.

In this section, we are going to look at three cases of trendline confluence.

1. Support level confluence
2. Resistance level confluence
3. Countertrend confluence

All of these cases use the trendline as the principal means of determining the trade setup while also ensuring that you enter or exit at the appropriate point. So, let's take a look at these setups in greater detail.

Support Level Confluence

In this type of setup, you are basically speculating on a breakout. Please bear in mind that you need to spot at least three hits in order to determine your support level. Additionally, the price action may reflect a resistance level, or perhaps not. It is not necessary to establish both a support and resistance level. The only requisite here is to establish a clear support level. In fact, if you see significant spikes, then you might be setting yourself up for a big gain.

Now, here is the most important part: the trendline needs to be located below the support level you have indicated. If the trend line is above the support level, you are too late. While you may still be able to ride the wave to the top, you can't expect to maximize your trade as you have gotten in after confluence, that is, the point in which the trendline officially intersects the support level. If you happen to get in right after confluence, you might be in for a big win. However, the later you get in, the greater your chances of missing out on the breakout.

To set up the trade, here's what you need:

First, clearly identify at least three points that indicate the support level. If there are more, then you are sure that's the bottom limit. This is the mark that you have a clear support level for the price action you are following.

Then, ensure that you have a rising trendline. This is important as a flat or falling trendline does not work for this case. If you identify the trendline emerging from a point in which there was a breakthrough, then you are poised for a significant increase.

Next, set your entry point at the expected support level point. This is the point in which you estimate the trendline will intersect with the support level. To simplify things, you can set this entry point automatically in your trade parameters. That way, the trade will only execute when the point is hit.

Lastly, set your stop-loss point at no more than 20 pips. This is important should the price plummet below the support level for whatever reason. Also, set your take-profit point depending on the risk to reward ratio you are using. For instance, if you perceive the gain to be massive, you can set up your risk to reward ratio at 1:3. So, if you set your stop-loss at 20 pips, you can set up your take-profit at 60 pips. This will lead you to a highly successful trade.

Note: if you exit the trade, but the price keeps rising, do not enter another trade. There is no telling the exact point in which the price will fall back down. So, it's best to sit out and what for the price to revert to mean. If you find that it doesn't touch the previous support level, then you might be seeing a new support level. Wait for a double bottom to confirm the possibility of a new support level and then repeat the same procedure.

Resistance Level Confluence

This type of trade is essentially the opposite of the support level confluence trade. The point of this trade is to avoid getting sucked into a falling price. This would not only zap your profits but may also leave you with a massive loss. So, it's best to make sure you have a good idea of what may happen.

In short, resistance level confluence is when you anticipate that a resistance level becomes a new support level. This is possible when the price plummets. While there is any number of reasons for this, you can use this type of trend to gain on the upswing. However, you are not anticipating that the price will go past the support level.

This is where you not only make money but also avoid getting hammered.

Here's how to set up this trade:

First, spot the support level of the price action you have been tracking. If there are multiple hits, then you can be relatively sure of this level. If there is a breakthrough with a reversion back to mean, then keep an eye on this as it could indicate a new support level.

Next, keep an eye on the original support level as this would be expected to become the new resistance level. This is due to the fact that the price will not necessarily revert to mean right away. Rather, it will hit the support level and then dip back down. This is the indication that the new resistance level has been hit.

Then, take a look at the trendline. Chances are the trendline will either be trading sideways (showing a horizontal move), or there will be a very slight upward or downward trend. If there is a clear upward or downward trend, then you are getting a false signal, as this could simply be an indication of volatility.

Lastly, follow the candlesticks. Check out the low point the price action hits before bouncing back up. When the price action hits the new resistance level and pops back down, you can set up your trade at the bottom and wait to cash in on the rebound.

With this trade, it's important to take care as you might enter the trade at what you observed to be the support level only to find that the price action broke through the floor. As such, you stand to get hammered. Please bear in mind that a sideways trendline is almost always a sure sign of this type of trade. Any other type of trendline will just be a false signal.

Countertrend Confluence

In this setup, you are working with a downward trend. As such, the main point here is to identify the resistance level as this point will indicate where you can expect the maximum profit to take place. Also, support levels are not particularly relevant. However, it would help to spot any double or triple bottoms so that you can ascertain where the low points may land. This can be used to help you set up your entry point.

Now, this setup is countertrend because the trendline is moving downward, yet you are looking to make money on the way back up once the price bounces back up off the floor. It should be noted that the platform will calculate a support level for you. So, a good rule of thumb in this setup is to make deals when the gap between the trendline and support level is the widest. This will enable a larger rebound. The shorter the gap between the trendline and the support level, the less money you stand to make. Additionally, you might be headed for a reversal. Thus, it might be best to sit this one out until you can spot the reversal.

To set up the trade, spot any double or triple tops. That will help you identify the points where you can expect the resistance level to be located. Then, look at the lows so you can set these up as your entry points. Last, set up your entry and exit points based on the lows and highs you have identified.

This strategy is quite useful if you are looking to make multiple trades in a single session. You may not get overwhelming returns, but this strategy will certainly help you get your feet firmly on the ground.

Stop Hunt Evasion

When investing in FOREX, it is always recommended that you set up stop-loss points in every trade. This is especially important when you are not planning to be at your terminal all the time. Some investors simply like to set up their trades and let the platform take care of the rest. That's why you need to set up stop-loss points on every single trade.

To do this, simply enter the price point for your stop loss below your entry point. Earlier, we recommended a stop-loss point of 20 pips. For instance, if your entry point is 10, you can set up your stop-loss at 9.80.

The reason for setting up a stop-loss below your entry lies in the hope that the price will rebound even though it has gone below your entry point. So, you can still capitalize on the upswing of the price. If the price does not rebound for any reason, you have cut your losses before they get out of hand.

Now, just as you have set up your stop-loss point, so has every other investor. You can assume that practically all investors have set up their stop-loss points within a reasonable level. This means that when the price suddenly plummets, a flood of stop-loss orders is triggered. This leads to a further price fall.

Some investors love to hunt for stop-loss orders in order to capitalize on lower-than-usual prices. This is called "stop hunting." To make money off this type of deal, you need to be keenly aware of the potential stop-loss points that other investors are setting up. Then, your aim is to capitalize on the stops so that you can catch the price of the currency pairing at the lowest possible point.

This is a highly speculative deal. This implies that you have no assurance that the price will rebound at the entry point you have selected. If anything, the price may still continue to go down further as the stop-loss orders continue to come in. Then, you might find yourself stuck in a position that's quickly falling in price. Then, there is no guarantee that the rebound will even get back to the entry position.

A good way of playing the "stop hunting" game is to play the countertrend strategy. Of course, you would need to be in the presence of a falling trendline (the stop-loss orders should reflect that). If this is the case, then you can expect a reasonable chance of the price rebounding at the support level for the currency pairing in question.

Stop hunting is not recommended for beginners. This is why you should first familiarize yourself with the various trend strategies we have outlined in this chapter. Afterward, you can make a reasonable assumption about the possible shifts in price so that you can set up your trades accordingly. While you can certainly make significant gains by stop hunting, please be sure to keep an eye out for false signals. These signals can be flashed when you see a high sell volume, but the trendline is moving upward. So, do keep an eye on the trading volume as this is the best indicator of a large number of stop-loss orders being triggered simultaneously.

CHAPTER 6

Introduction To And Rules Of Divergence

Divergence is one of the most common indicators which is used to guide investment decisions. When you are able to spot divergence clearly, you can pick up on the overall direction a trend is heading. In this manner, you can anticipate, within a reasonable margin, the potential reversal in trend.

When you go about using divergence as a means of setting up your trading strategy, it's important to note that you can profit from either a bullish or bearish trend. It all depends on how soon you are able to spot the potential reversal, as indicated by the trend itself.

That is why this chapter is focused on using divergence as a strategy so that you can set up your deals quickly and effectively. The main thing to keep in mind is that you need to spot the divergence so that you can take advantage of it.

In most books on trading, you'll find that divergence is determined by the interaction between trend and the moving average. This technique is commonly referred to as MACD (moving average convergence divergence).

In the MACD strategy, what you are essentially doing is spotting the points in which the moving average is going to intersect with the trendline. While this technique is highly effective, it may lead to possible false signals as the moving average is just one measure of what you can expect as a means of calculating the overall trend pattern of the currency pair you are tracking.

In this chapter, we are going to use Price Action as a means of determining divergence so that you can have a clear and accurate picture of when reversals are about to take place. You will find that this is the most effective way of determining divergence so that you can set up entry and exit points. Best of all, you are not using any additional measures beyond the most reliable indicator there is price.

When going about divergence as a strategy, there are some helpful tips to keep in mind:

- Make sure that highs and higher than the previous high and that lows are lower than the previous low. This means that when spotting divergence, your highs need to break out, and the lows need to break through. When you spot there, you'll be able to get the right tracking for the divergence you seek. Double tops and bottoms are the best way for you to spot this.

- Tops and bottoms need to be in successive order. This means that you must spot sharp dips and spikes. It won't work if you have smaller dips and spikes; all you might be seeing is an increased amount of trading volume.

- Ensure that the trendline is on the right path to intersect with the tops or bottoms you are looking at. Otherwise, you might be getting in too soon or too late. This is important as the reversal will take place at the point where the trendline intersects with a major top or major bottom.

- Also, please ensure that you look at different timeframes. If you focus only on tone timeframe, you'll be missing the entire picture. Please bear in mind that anything can happen in a short time period. So, it's always best to go back further in time to confirm your strategy. That way, you can be reasonably sure that you are on the right path.

Using Divergence for Entry and Exit Strategies

Divergence is highly effective when you are looking to plot entry and exit points as part of your overall trading strategy. Mainly divergence can signal at what point you can get in and at what point you should get out. It should be noted that the perfect entry point is the lowest possible point during a bearish trend. In contrast, the ideal point to get out would be the highest possible point during a bullish trend. In either of these cases, you would ideally get in or out right before the change in trend takes place. This is what can allow you to maximize your profit either way. So, let's take a look at how you can capitalize on this situation.

First, let's start with a bearish trend.

By definition, a bearish trend implies that the overall price action is trending downward. Even if you have significant spikes along the way, you can determine your trendline to be a downward slope. When this occurs, you need to spot when the trend will reverse.

The main point of playing a bearish trend is trying to determine the entry point of a trade setup. As such, you are looking to find the lowest possible point, right before the trend is about to reverse. Theoretically, this is the point where the trendline intersects with the lowest point of the price action. However, this point needs to be at least at the lowest point of the support level.

Consequently, the first step toward making this strategy work is to clearly identify the support level. A double bottom would be a great indicator that this setup will work effectively. You might try to go on a single breakthrough. However, that's not enough confirmation that the trend will reverse. That would constitute a false signal. Therefore, a double bottom is the best indicator. If you happen to see a triple bottom without the trendline intersecting, then you are getting ready for a huge takeoff.

Your entry point will be revealed when you spot the exact intersection of the trendline with the support level. This is where you can enter the trade. Then, you can expect the price to take off. The exit point is determined by your risk to reward ratio. You can set your exit anywhere from 20 to 60 pips above your entry. However, it would be recommended that you double check previous highs. This will give you the best indication as to where you can reasonably expect the high to hit.

Now, let's take a look at this strategy based on a bullish trend.

The whole point of this strategy is to figure out the best exit point. This exit point is intended to maximize your profit. Thus, the objective is to leave the trade at the highest possible point right before the trend reverses.

To do this, it's important to identify the resistance level. Ideally, you would have a double top you can use as a reference point. If you have a double top in which one of the points broke out of the resistance level band, then you may be seeing a false signal. This is generally due to increased trading volume. To make this setup work appropriately, you need to make sure that the double top stays at or very close to the resistance level. If you cannot spot a breakout after a triple top, then the downtrend will be quite sharp. So, it might be a good idea for you to set up your exit point slightly before the resistance level limit.

In both cases, it's important to automatically setup stop-loss and take-profit points as this will ensure that you don't fall asleep at the wheel. This is especially important if you don't plan to be physically present at your terminal. In such cases, the market orders will be triggered automatically once your specific point is triggered. Please keep in mind that setting up your take-profit and stop-loss points automatically will save you a lot of headaches further down the road.

Handling Divergence Drawdown

One of the biggest challenges that FOREX investors face when utilizing the divergence strategy is drawdown. Drawdown occurs when a number of stops are triggered at various points in a trading cycle. When a sudden number of stops are hit, the price may automatically tank, thereby leaving investors short of profit. In fact, sudden drawdown may trigger further stops.

This is why it's very common to find sudden dips in price. It's not so much that there has been a sudden shift in investor psyche; the fact is that when a number of stops are triggered all at once, the market automatically reacts. When the price dips and further stops are triggered, it can be hard to make a profit.

Unfortunately, some investors find that their positions are liquidated even before they get into take-profit territory. All of this is due to the fact that stops are triggered automatically.

Now, here is a common mistake that investors make: they decide to avoid setting up automatic stop-loss points in order to avoid being liquidated in a drawdown. This is a dangerous situation, to say the least. There is no doubt that you are playing with fire. It could be that the action gets hot and heavy, really fast. As such, you may not have enough time to react. This is why you cannot expect your human reflexes to react faster than a computer.

It's also important to note that divergence trading is not an exact science. Because of the fact that stops can suddenly be triggered all at once, you have to be aware that it is by no means a perfect strategy. This is why setting up your deal in the right manner will help you avoid getting knocked out of the game even before you have a chance to make a profit.

It should also be noted that you need to ensure to keep your instincts in check. If you choose to set up your take-profit points to high, you may not have a chance to get that high. As a result, you'll be knocked out by sudden drawdowns.

Now, there is one other thing to watch out for: if you get in at the bottom of the trend, it means that your stop-loss point will be much lower than that of an investor who got in after you did. As a result, managing an adequate risk to reward ratio will help you manage drawdowns much easier.

Consider this situation:

You got it right at the bottom of the trend, right before it reversed. As such, your position is now 1. You decided to set up your stop at 20 pips. This would set your stop-loss 0.80

while you are using a risk to reward ratio of 2:1. Consequently, you set your take-profit mark will be 1.40 (20 pips * 2 – this is the 2:1 ratio).

Under this setup, let's assume that the price hits 1.41, then your position will be liquidated as you hit your automatic take-profit mark. This means a successful trade. You make money, and all is good. However, let's assume that you are feeling bold. You set up a 3:1 risk to reward ratio. This puts your take-profit point at 1.60. However, as investors get in later, they set up their stops at around 1.45. A sudden dip in the price at around 1.47 causes prices to dip below 1.45. This automatically triggers a bunch of stops. A number of positions are liquidated, and the price does not make it past 1.40. Yet, you are stuck with a take-profit point of 1.60.

Do you see why you may never hit your take-profit point if you set it too high?

This is why savvy investors know that it's best to set up trades that are realistic. If the price of the currency pairing seems to be trending at a maximum of 1.50, for instance, then you might be better off setting up your take profit point somewhere below this range. This will ensure that you avoid setting up your expectations too high, thereby running the risk of leaving you out in the cold.

Avoiding Divergence Drawdown

The easiest way to avoid divergence drawdown is to look at the resistance level for the currency pairing you are tracking. While you might be tempted to set up your take-profit point right at the top of the wave, you might think twice about it. If you see a double top, then a reversal might be upon you. In this case, it might be best to set up your exit point slightly below that mark. Even 5 pips can make a difference.

Another important way in which you can avoid drawdown is to anticipate it. You can tell a drawdown is on the horizon where there is a high volume of trading. If you see that there is a large number of trades happening at one time, you might be keen to keep an eye. If you see that the price has leveled off, sell immediately. The sooner you can liquidate your position, the greater the profit you will make. This is important as it will enable you to make a reasonable profit rather than see it get zapped by the sudden flood of stops. While this depends on your reaction time, it's usually a good way of avoiding your profits being zapped altogether.

Lastly, a good way to avoid drawdowns is to play it safe. If you liquidate your position well before the trend reverses, then you might consider re-entering the play, except this time with a much tighter position, say a 1:1 risk to reward ratio, just to be on the safe side.

How to Identify the Right Divergence Setups

Identifying divergence setups can be tricky. Thus far, we have gone over the main points that are needed in order to properly determine a potential divergence setup. So, it's important to go over the possible false signals that you may encounter when researching a setup.

The first false signal to watch out for is a trendline that does not figure to intersect the resistance or support level. So, you may have double or even triple tops and bottoms but no trendline to intersect. Now, you might be tempted to think that there might be a reversal, for instance, when looking for an entry point. However, you may find that a breakthrough is much likelier in a situation such as this.

Another false signal to watch out for is a trendline that is moving sideways. This is a very dangerous point to get into. If you are not careful, you might end up getting into a trade that will leave you missing out. When you have a sideways trendline, always be on the lookout for the candlesticks. If you see that the candlesticks are point toward a downturn, then be ready to exit. In this case, you may set up at a very tight stop and profit point, say, 10 pips either way. This is the type of setup in which you are looking to make a quick profit and leave.

Lastly, another false signal is when you do not see a clear trend. You may have double or triple tops and bottoms, but no clearly define trendline. In this case, the trendline may look like a wave or may have very sharps spikes and dips. This could be the result of an increased level of trading activity. It may just indicate that stock investors, for instance, are moving into FOREX as a means of getting away from stocks for a while. So, please try to avoid using the just tops and bottoms as a means of guiding your setup. You need to keep an eye on the trendline. Otherwise, you may enter a deal based on a false signal. While you may get lucky, the likelihood is just as great for you to lose.

Divergence and Confluence

Confluence occurs when two or more indicators meet each other at some point in a chart. This means that you need to look at various indicators to ensure that you have the right setup in mind. To do this type of analysis, the most common means is through the MACD.

In this type of strategy, you need to use the moving average of the currency pair you are trading. In this regard, the MACD will enable you to visualize the moving average of the price in question in addition to the price action. If you have both of these indicators moving together toward a point of intersection, then you have confluence. When they are moving away from one another, then you have divergence. Both of these scenarios are useful in helping you spot where your next move may lie.

Let's look at confluence first.

Confluence occurs when you have a price action trendline and moving average getting closer to one another. In the event that you have a bearish trendline and a bullish moving average, then you are seeing a potential reversal in trend. The reversal occurs at the point in which the two lines intersect. The point in which they ought to intersect should be somewhere at or near the support level. Once the lines have intersected with one another, they will begin to move away. It's important to watch out for the point in which they may hit the support level as the absences of clear bottoms may be more indicative of a breakthrough rather than a reversal in trend.

Now, let's look at divergence.

In the event of divergence, you have both the price action trendline and the moving average creating a gap. For instance, you have a bearish moving average and a bullish price action trendline. What this indicates is that the price action is slowing down. As such, it is a warning to avoid getting in at the wider points of the gap. If anything, you may want to look at liquidating your positions as prices may soon begin to level off. This would serve as a clear indication that it's time to sell. If the price action is getting closer to your take-profit level, just make sure you don't have any sudden drawdowns.

Using Bollinger Bands in Divergence Trading

Bollinger Bands is a trading strategy in which you have price action moving within a predictable band or range. This means that the price moves up to a resistance level and then falls back down to a support level before rising back up again. This type of trading is rather predictable and a great way of making steady earnings. This may not be the sexiest way of making money, but it sure is effective.

When using Bollinger Bands, the moving average is your best tool. You can track the trendline for the moving average in such a way that you can clearly determine the resistance and support levels. Consequently, divergence helps you to spot the exact points at which you ought to get in and the point at which you need to exit.

In short, Bollinger Bands set up both resistance and support levels based on successive hits on resistance and support levels. However, to use this strategy correctly, you need to identify at least three hits on both the support and resistance levels without any sign of breakout or breakthrough.

Additionally, you need to use a longer timeframe, say 48 hours, to truly identify this pattern. While this pattern is relatively common, especially among correlated pairs, it is important to note that the price action trendline will move up or down based on the moving average trend. So, your goal is to identify the exact point in which the reversal in trend will occur. At that point, you exit the trade, collect your profits, and then wait for the price action to move back down close to the resistance level and then back up again.

As stated earlier, Bollinger Bands are not the most exciting way of making a profit, but it allows you to make predictable earnings that you can count on to help you reach your investment goals.

Psychological Levels

For all the data and analytics in the world, investors are usually driven by psychological factors. These factors may range from fundamental elements such as economic stability to purely subjective factors like expectations.

As such, psychological levels are generally associated with resistance and support levels. For instance, investors may set up a round number as a particular threshold that must be crossed in order for them to buy or sell.

Consider this situation:

A currency pair has been trading in a predictable Bollinger Band. The price fluctuates from a high of 1.48 to a low of 1.41. As such, investors may not feel compelled to act out given the fact that there are very few incentives to make any large moves. This is due to the fact that investors see the 1.50 mark as a threshold. If the price moves past this point, they will sell. This would then trigger a flood of sell orders and knock the price back down. In contrast, investors will begin dumping their positions if the price falls through the 1.40 mark.

It should be noted that there may be no technical reasoning for this psychological expectation. However, investors have seen these round numbers, 1.40 and 1.50, as milestones that will dictate their ultimate reactions. This is why technical analysis should become your new best friend. Without it, you are left with subjective assessments that may have no real foundation for them. As a result, you might not make the best investment decisions. However, if your psychological perception is based on technical data, then you have a very good chance of making sound investment decisions and subjective assessments based on hard data.

Risk Management in Divergence Trading

Risk is an investor's worst enemy. Simply put, the greater the risk, the greater the chance you will lose money. This is why managing risk is so important when it comes to successful trading. On the whole, you can manage risk by paying close attention to the data. The more you study the data, the easier it will become for you to spot trends simply by looking at charts. Often, these charts will tell you everything you need to know. You won't even have to consult any expert advice. The combination of data, experience, and instinct will be enough to guide you.

That being said, here are some useful tips to keep in mind when managing risk.

- First, avoid committing too much in a single trade. Even if the trade setup looks perfect, it's always best to avoid committing too much money in one trade. The level of risk skyrockets the more money you put into a single trade. So, keeping the 1% to 2% rule in mind will save you from making a terrible mistake. This is especially important when you are first starting out.

- Second, avoid making deals based on false signals. Always look for all of the signs before entering a trade. If there is a signal missing or if you are unsure, then don't enter the trade. It's better to see you missed out on an opportunity rather than regret getting in. There will always be another opportunity.

- Third, play it safe. It is always best to err on the side of caution. If you find that the setup is perfect, committing 2% of your investment capital will be more than enough to validate your thoughts.

- Lastly, diversification is key. Most successful investors have multiple positions open in various currency pairs. This allows you to manage risk more effectively as you are not dependent on the action of a single currency. When you spread risk out among various currencies, you reduce the likelihood of missing out greatly. So, do your best to enter multiple positions in various pairs. That way, the losses from one deal can be offset by the winnings of another.

On the whole, risk management boils down to using common sense. When you follow the data and use your good judgment, you will find that missing out on a deal would be tough. You won't miss out on any good deals. Rather, you'll stay on the right side of your mistakes. While you will not have a perfect streak, the likelihood of you getting wiped out will be far less. That is why keeping the various guidelines provided in this chapter will ensure that you will come out on top more often than not.

CHAPTER 7

Risk Management In The Forex Market

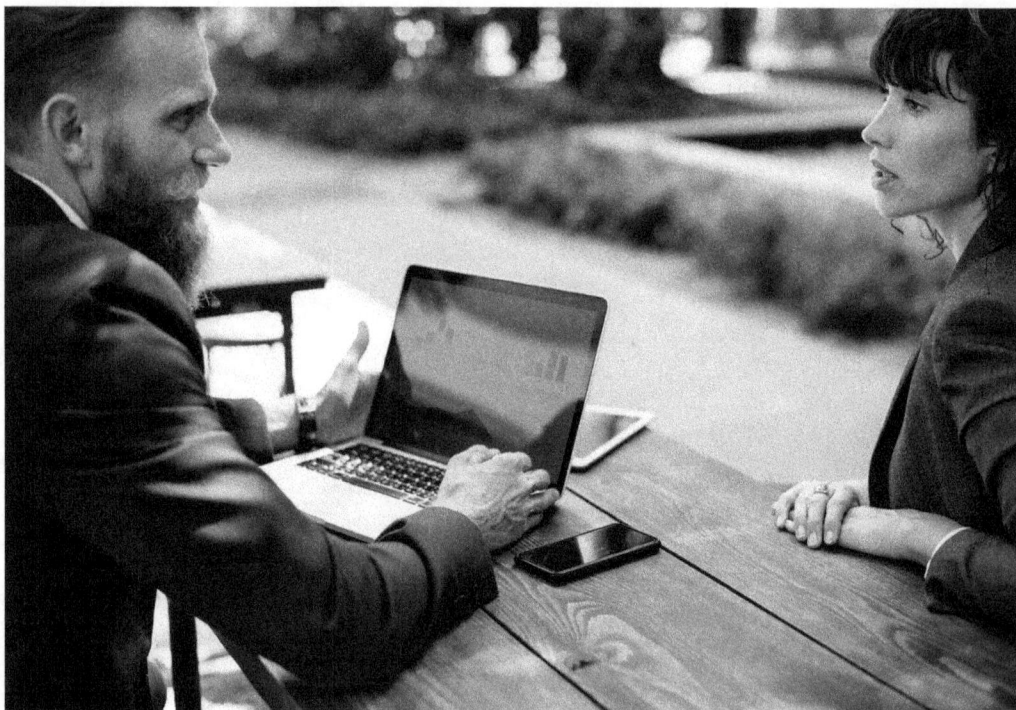

When investing, risk is a fundamental factor that you need to take into account. If you choose to take on too much risk, you open the door for potential disaster. While that may sound a little over the top, the fact is that risk is a constant in any investment environment. As a result, it's imperative that you take the necessary steps to ensure that you make the best investment decision based on the information you have available at the moment.

Managing risk boils down to making sound investment decisions based on technical data. Whenever you base your decisions on subjective valuations, you risk making assessments based on incomplete information. This can lead you to miscalculate the circumstances under which you have evaluated your position. Consequently, risk management requires you to make a very detailed assessment based on technical analysis.

Now, it's important to keep in mind that if you don't have enough information to make an educated assessment, it might be best for you to sit out the action until you have enough information. As we have pointed out at various points throughout this book, it's best to err on the side of caution. When you strive to play it safe, especially in the early going, then you can be sure that you won't make any rash decisions that might put your position at risk.

That being said, it's also important to consider that if you have a higher risk tolerance, then it's worth considering that more aggressive moves require you to be even more studious of the data in front of you. Indeed, the large amount of data can be overwhelming at times. Nevertheless, it's totally worth plowing through the data. It's the safest way for you to learn the ropes of the FOREX market.

Earlier, we mentioned that MetaTrader 4 provides you with options that enable you to literally copy trades. With this option, you can study successful trades. In a manner of speaking, this is a type of reverse engineering which can allow you to make the most of the situation. Consequently, you won't have to struggle in the early going. You'll be able to see how successful deals are set up for yourself.

Ultimately, these types of setups can help you to identify your own setups. This is crucial as learning the ropes of the FOREX market boils down to ensuring that you have the right initiation. When you have the fundamentals down, the risk is reduced exponentially. By the same token, if you don't have any clarity with the fundamentals, then you are only asking for trouble.

That is why we are going to focus this chapter on the best way in which you can manage risk so that you can ensure a successful outcome with the majority of your trades. While we can't ensure that you will win every trade (if only that were possible!), we can ensure that you won't set yourself up for any catastrophic deals. This will help you build your portfolio to a point in which you will feel confident, making the most out of your trading endeavors.

Picking the Right Broker for You

Picking the right broker for you can be a daunting task, especially if you are not clear and what you should be looking for. On the whole, finding a good broker isn't too hard when you know what you are looking for.

However, the question begs: why do you need a broker in the first place?

This is a reasonable question. The reason why you need a broker in order to enter the FOREX market is that you, as an individual, are not officially permitted to trade in the FOREX market unless you have the backing of a licensed institution. In this case, the brokerage firms that offer access to their platforms are the institutions that will back your trading activity.

In a manner of speaking, it's like you're playing your home games in someone else's stadium. It's still your home turf even though you don't actually own the stadium. In this regard, the access you are granted to the platform enables you to place trades for yourself. All you pay to the brokerage firm is the right to use their platform.

That's all.

So, you aren't hiring a broker to manage your portfolio. What you are doing is simply "paying to play." A good way of looking at it is by comparing it to poker. When you play professional poker, you need to buy your way into the game. This is in addition to the blind you have to pay for each hand. Similarly, FOREX platforms will charge you for the access to enter the platform. Once you are in, then you can place your trades with the trading capital you have at your disposal. This will then enable you to make a profit.

The best part of this type of setup is that the profits you make are yours. You don't have to pay a commission to some broker for their "expertise." By reading this book, among other publications out there, you will gain the same type of knowledge that brokers have. Therefore, you won't have to waste your money by paying commissions. That goes straight into your pocket.

As such, there are some important points to consider when looking for a brokerage firm that can grant you access to the FOREX market.

1. **Membership fees**. All FOREX trading platforms will charge you some kind of membership fee. This fee is generally used to keep the platform running. Thus, the price you pay is what basically keeps the lights on. Regular brokerage firms will charge you a flat fee for the use of the platform. This can either be an annual fee or a recurring monthly payment. In other cases, discount brokers may charge you a one-time signup fee. However, they'll get you on the back end with their fees per trade. When you opt for a full-service broker, you'll pay a higher upfront fee, but you'll get a great analytics package that offsets the cost of the platform itself. Also, depending on the type of platform, you get algorithmic trading, expert advice, and even the opportunity to do copy-cat trading. Most discount brokers simply offer you access to the platform, and that's it.

2. **Fees per trade**. When you conduct individual trades, you generally end up paying a fee per trade. In some cases, you may end up paying a couple of bucks on each trade regardless of the size of the position. In other cases, you pay pennies per trade. The best way to maximize your value when it comes to fees per trade is to purchase bundles. Most platforms offer bundle packs like 10 trades for $1.99. These offer the most value as they allow you to control your expenses. If you go on a trade-by-trade basis, you'll find it hard to keep tabs on the amount of money you are paying per trade. So, it's best to see if you can lock in the price you pay for each trade you place.

3. **Reputation**. This is one of the most important aspects to consider. Sure, you might be tempted by the neat look offered by Joe's Trading Platform. But if you don't have any idea of who they are, you might be walking into a scam. The best trading platforms have a good reputation backing them. In addition, you'll find plenty of independent reviews on them by regular folks. You can even call up the Better Business Bureau in your area and get information on the parent company. Legit companies are always in the business of transparency as they know how valuable a good reputation can be.

4. **Free demo account**. This is a deal-breaker. If a platform does not offer you a free demo account, then it's better if you pass on them, at least in the early going. When you don't have access to the free demo version, then you will be playing for real right from the start. This can be dangerous, particularly when you don't have a lot of experience. So, a demo account will always be your best bet. Most platforms will require a credit card number or some other type of payment option though they won't bill you until after the trial period has ended. Take full advantage of this time as you are playing with house money. Therefore, you can afford to make a few mistakes. That way, you know what to look out for when you live with the real thing.

Please keep these points in mind as they will save you a lot of headaches along the way. In particular, ensuring that you are dealing with a reputable company is the most important thing you can do to protect yourself from unnecessary risk.

Signs of a Legitimate Broker

When you are selecting the brokerage firm you plan to do business with; there are a number of signs you can look out for. So, let's take a look at these signs:

1. You can get full information on the parent company running the platform. This is a biggie. If you cannot find out who's behind the platform, then you are better off staying away from them. When you know who is running the show in the background, then you can rest assured you are dealing with pros. The main issue to keep in mind is that not being sure of who you are dealing with can lead you to give your money to unlicensed firms. This will not only result in you losing your money, but you may also end up sharing sensitive personal information.

2. They are licensed. This is another important thing to consider. If the firm you are dealing with cannot produce any official licensing information, then you had better run away as fast as you can. Please keep in mind that platforms pop up every so often. Now, they might be licensed for a while. But after the scam enough people, they lose their licensing. Yet, they advertise themselves as if they were duly licensed. So, a cursory check at their licensing information should provide you with the assurance you need. In particular, a walk through the Securities and Exchange Commission's (SEC) website should provide you with the assurance you seek.

3. The price makes sense. When you are dealing with officially licensed firms, the price will reflect this. While we're not saying that it will be expensive, we are saying

that the price will be on par with the market. This is why you need to beware of prices that are too good to be true. Of course, there is always the chance that you are dealing with promos. However, the price should be a major tip-off.

4. There are plenty of reviews about them. Whether they are good or bad, you will find a good number of reviews about them. Users will be happy to leave both good and bad comments if given a chance. As such, finding a good amount of comments about them will help you determine if they are right for you. In contrast, if you can't find any information on them, then you might very well be dealing with a fraudulent company. This is why user feedback is so important.

5. They have an active presence on social media. If they are legit, you'll find them all over social media. Consequently, you will also find a number of user reviews and conversations about them. This is a great way of knowing who you're really dealing with. Even if they are new in the market, you'll them making an effort to gain traction on social media. In some cases, legitimate brokers will go out of their way to ensure engagement. Such efforts are always a positive sign.

Signs of an Illegitimate Broker

When you're shopping for a brokerage firm to grant you access to the market, it might be tempting to go with the cheapest option you can find. At first, this may seem like a good idea, but one the whole, please bear in mind that you get what you pay for. So, here are the most important signs to watch out for when looking to spot illegitimate brokers.

1. They don't offer a demo account. This is a key issue when it comes to determining if you are dealing with a legit broker. Any time you sign on for a new account, you should get a chance to try out the platform for free during a short trial period. This period is generally 15 days though it could be longer depending on the type of promotion the company may be running. In some cases, you may get a full access 7-day pass. As long as you get the free trial period, you can rest assured that you'll have the chance to test the entire system out first and then make up your mind. If the broker asks for money upfront, then you may be getting yourself in trouble.

2. They don't disclose their licensing information. This is an automatic deal-breaker. If you can't get any information on their licensing, then it's best to just get away from their platform. Clever scammers may appear to sell you access to a platform, but you might find out that it's just a test platform or some other type of demo software that doesn't actually trade the real thing. So, you might get scammed into believing you are really trading when you're really not. Also, you may be dealing with a once reputable broker that either has an expired license or a revoked one. So, make sure you do your homework on this one.

3. They don't provide any information about their leadership or board members. When you're dealing with legitimate companies, they are generally publicly traded firms. As such, this type of information is available on their website. You can easily find out who's on their board and what type of credentials they have. Additionally, you can find links to social media pages like LinkedIn. While this isn't exactly a

guarantee either, illegitimate brokers are usually scant with the amount of information they provide.

4. You can't find information on the financial institution backing them. Whether it's a financial institution such as an investment firm or a bank, you'll be able to easily get information on who's running the platform. If the platform is not clear about this, they are trying to scam you, plain and simple. By getting information on the institution supporting the platform, you can then decide if you'd like to do business with them or not.

5. They are little to no reviews. Some of them are clearly fake, too. Social media is really good at exposing scammers. If you find that their social media sites are filled with glowing reviews, that should serve as a red flag. Additionally, it's important to keep in mind that there will always be unhappy folks. So, a balanced amount of positive and negative comments should provide you with enough food for thought. Also, if positive comments appear to be coming from fake profiles, then you have an idea of what you're dealing with.

Money Management in FOREX Investing

Learning about money management in the world of FOREX is an essential tool that will help you steer clear of trouble. Mainly, money management pertains to a set of principles that you can apply when making investment decisions. These rules enable you to build a discipline that can help you to protect your investment capital while maximizing your potential for profit and gain.

So, here are 10 rules which can help you make the most of your investment dollars in the FOREX market.

1. **Stay clear of any software, programs, or platforms that guarantee results**. This goes without saying. Nothing is guaranteed in life. Yet, you will find that there are programs and companies that tout their platforms, programs, systems, and so on as guaranteed money-makers. The only thing that can guarantee you solid results is good, old-fashioned study and dedication to trading. Please be careful as so-called gurus and experts may offer you the keys to the kingdom for a low price. These are generally scams that, in the best of cases, will only leave you with subpar results. So, please be wary of any trading system that offers amazing returns in a short time period.

2. **Make use of a demo account**. Any reputable FOREX platform will offer you a free demo account loaded with monopoly money. Make sure that you take full advantage of this account. Not only will it help you to learn the ropes of the platform itself, but you can also practice as much as you can without the worry of losing any real money. If anything, you can go wild and try out any number of strategies before going live. There is no better way for you to learn how to trade without the risk of losing your initial investment. We have mentioned this point several times. It is so important that it's part of the rules of money management.

3. **Avoid involving emotions**. This is arguably the most important rule. The reasoning behind this rule is that getting emotionally involved can backfire on you.

Whether you are winning or losing, when emotions get the best of you, you open up yourself to taking on risk you normally wouldn't take. So, if you are upset after losing out on a deal, it might be best to push back from the table and take a break. There is nothing with catching a breather, especially when things aren't going your way. Please remember that keeping a level head when trading in any market is one of the cornerstones to making sound investment decisions. Sure, we are all human and get emotional. But if you let your emotions dictate your strategies, then you might be setting yourself up for trouble down the road.

4. **Don't be stingy on a good education**. When it comes to studying FOREX, don't cut corners with your time and your efforts. You don't have to spend a great deal of money. All you need is to invest time and effort into learning as much as you can about investing in FOREX. Most importantly, please keep in mind that this is an ongoing process. Books such as this one, are a valuable means of improving your trading acumen. There are also other publications that you can provide you with information that can be useful at any given point. Additionally, there are training courses out there which you can take on major learning platforms. These courses are not endorsed by any specific platform or broker. So, you can be certain that you are going to receive unbiased information.

5. **Being successful at FOREX is something that you can learn**. Being successful at FOREX isn't something that you can just pop out of a box. While it takes time to master the market, it is something that you can totally learn. That is why no system can guarantee to be foolproof. While you can use systems out there

as a guide, you need to take the time to make sure it's the right system for you. Please keep in mind that all skills are learnable. If you have the chance to learn from experienced pros, so much the better. The main point here is to make learning a lifelong journey. You will find that there is so much more to learn in the world of investing. In fact, don't be surprised to find that when you thought you knew everything there was to know, something else comes up that expands your current knowledge base.

6. **Manage your funds wisely**. A good rule of thumb is to never invest more than 2% of your investment capital on a single deal. When you do this, the problem is that it opens up the door to a great deal of trouble. For example, if you go all-in on a single deal, you run the risk of blowing your entire capital. This would not only be devastating, but you would be broke afterward. Please take care of your investment capital as much as possible. Even if you are just starting out with a few hundred dollars, your investment capital is highly valuable. So, blowing it all irresponsibly makes no sense. The 2% rule is an iron law that will help keep you in the race all the time.

7. **Spread the wealth**. While you might feel comfortable trading certain currencies, it's important to branch out and explore other potential currencies. You might be surprised to find that there is money to be made in various types of currencies. Often, most investors overlooked hidden gems such as those countries whose currency is gaining value. This is why fundamental analysis is always a great way you can sniff out a potential deal. Please keep in mind that diversification is the

name of the game. This is especially true when you're dealing with uncorrelated pairs. You will find that these pairs offer the best hedge against the risk that comes with putting all of your eggs into a single basket.

8. **Common sense always wins**. When you look at potential deals, or experts claiming to have magical formulas to great returns, use your common sense. This is especially true when you think about something being "too good to be true." In such cases, common sense would dictate a more cautious approach. In addition, if you have a gut instinct telling you that something is not right, it's always best to err on the side of caution. If you find that the data just doesn't seem to back your assumptions, then you might be better off sitting on the sidelines. In FOREX, it's better to prove yourself that you were right, even though you didn't get into the trade as opposed to getting in just to find out you were wrong. The good part about sitting out is that you then have experience which can serve later on.

9. **Hedge risk as much as possible**. The use of stop-loss orders must become your new go-to device whenever you enter a deal. The use of stop-loss orders will cap your losses up to a certain point. This will keep you from being wiped out in case a deal should happen to go sour at any point. This is why we keep reminding investors over and over about the importance of implementing stop-loss and take-profits points all the time. You might be tempted to take the auto-pilot off and fly solo, but please bear in mind that action can get hot and heavy. As a result, you may not have enough time to react. As such, you may end up losing out simply because you didn't react fast enough.

Take care of overusing leverage. This is another one of those risky strategies that you need to keep in mind. When you make heavily leveraged deals, you are opening the door for disaster. So, make sure that if you do use leverage, you have found a manageable level that would ensure you don't get wiped out should something not go right.

With these golden rules, you will come out ahead most of the time. While there are no guarantees in any market, you can be sure that you will have a good chance to come out ahead every time. So, do take the time to go over these rules again and again until they become second nature to you. In the end, you'll find that the combination of theory and practical experience will help you build the killer instinct you need to be successful in the FOREX trading market. Ultimately, all the skills you need are perfectly learnable. Thus, please devote as much time as you can to learning and building upon your current skills.

CHAPTER 8

Analysis & Trade Sharing

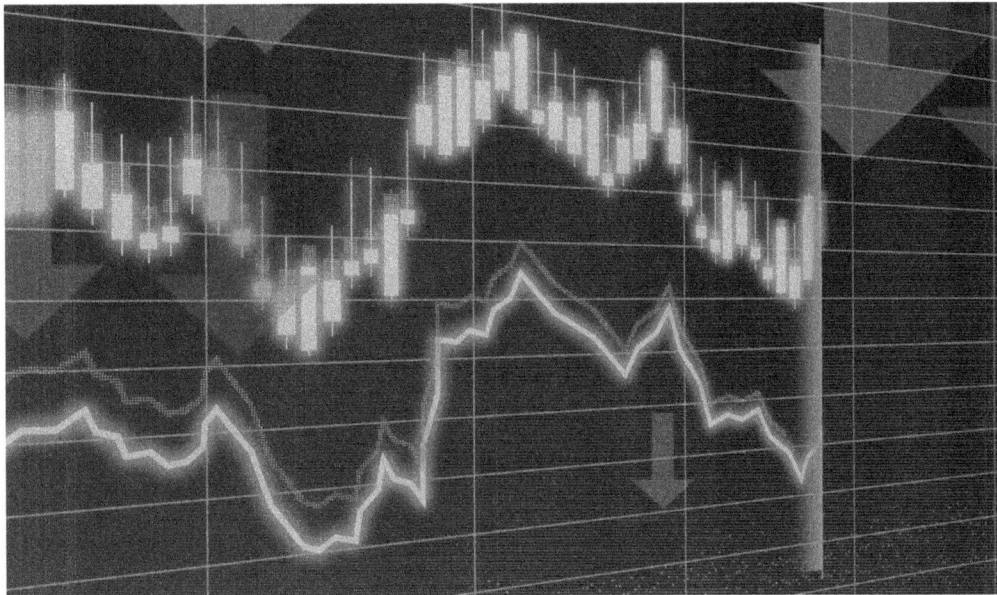

In the rule of money management, we mentioned investor psychology as a crucial factor to consider. Indeed, your mentality plays a critical role in establishing a winning attitude during your trading activities. Those investors who are able to keep their emotions in check are the ones who can maintain a more balanced approach. Those who cannot keep their emotions in check often find themselves making deals they later regret.

Let's consider an example of this situation.

When you make a bad deal and lose money, you might be tempted to "double down." When you double down, you are essentially going "double or nothing." Needless to say, the risk that's involved in this type of deal grows exponentially the more you double down.

Now, it's one thing to lose $100 and double down on that. However, if you lose $100, then lose $200, double down on $400, and so on, you are taking on completely unnecessary risk. Unless $100 represents 1% of your investment capital, it's best to let it go. You will be able to offset those losses with the profits you make from other deals.

In fact, when you double down, you are increasing the likelihood of failure exponentially.

How so?

Please take a look at the following chart:

Investment Capital	% Lost	$ Lost	Remaining Balance	% Gain Required to Break Even
$1,000	-5.00%	$50	$950	5.26%
$1,000	-10.00%	$100	$900	11.11%
$1,000	-20.00%	$200	$800	25.00%
$1,000	-30.00%	$300	$700	42.86%

$1,000	-40.00%	$400	$600	66.67%
$1,000	-50.00%	$500	$500	100.00%
$1,000	-60.00%	$600	$400	150.00%
$1,000	-70.00%	$700	$300	233.33%
$1,000	-80.00%	$800	$200	400.00%
$1,000	-90.00%	$900	$100	900.00%
$1,000	-95.00%	$900	$50	1,900.00%

In this chart, we can see how the more money you put into a trade, the more money you need to double down in order to recoup your losses. So, if you start off with a $1,000 investment and lose $50 of it, you only need to profit 5% in your next deal to make your money back. However, if you were to invest half of it, that is $500, you would need to double your money on subsequent deals in order to break even. If you invest $900, you need to make a 1,900% profit just to make your money back. Naturally, this is an unrealistic amount of money to make. You might be able to make that type of return over a series of successful deals (rather tough, though not impossible). Ultimately, this is not the best strategy to keep in mind.

As you can see, this is why keeping your emotions in check is a valuable tip you can put into practice. If you let greed get the better of you, you may not be able to recover from a mistake. By the same token, if you get sucked into the doubling-down game, you may not be able to pull yourself out of the hole. Moreover, if you decide to double down using leverage, you may very well end up getting banned from the platform if you are unsuccessful.

Now, you might be thinking, "what if I am successful?"

That is a very dangerous situation. It could lead to a false sense of security. You might think you are really smart when you were just lucky. Of course, we are not doubting your skills and intelligence. However, doubling down on a deal is so risky. It can lead to any number of possible situations in which you risk losing your entire investment capital. As a result, it's always best to err on the side of caution. You never know what can happen. Thus, it's best to be on the safe side, especially in the early going.

Developing a Solid Trading Mindset

Throughout this book, we have emphasized the importance of solid technical analysis and objective data. However, a good mindset is just as important. This implies that having a good mindset can be just as important as maintaining a close watch on the technical data that you need to place successful trades.

Often, novice investors get sucked into a silly game. This game consists of the Hollywood version of what an investor should be. Many times, Hollywood films depict investors and brokers as overly aggressive individuals who are arrogant and egocentric. Moreover, these films make it seem like you have to be pushy and go to extremes to make money.

What these films don't generally depict is that becoming a successful investor or broker isn't about being the toughest or meanest kid on the block. Being a successful investor is about learning to take your lumps in stride while using your head to make sound investment decisions. When you are able to make decisions based on reliable data, you can filter out the negative emotions that come with investing.

What negative emotions are we talking about?

Here are some to consider:

- **Fear**. This is by far your biggest enemy. Fear can compel you to act irrationally while also cause you to freeze. For example, when the market is a sudden downturn, investors panic and begin dumping their positions. This leads to bargains that can be scooped up later. So, a good rule of thumb to consider is that when others are liquidating their positions, look for bargains you can scoop up. Who knows what goodies you can find on the cheap?

- **Greed**. It's easy to fall for greed when you have a string of successful trades. You might go on a roll and make a killing. This can lead to a false sense of security. You might even think that you have it all figured out. And while that may be true, the problem lies in the fact that you take on unnecessary risk. Herein lies the problem. If you think you have everything down cold and decide to take on more and more risk, you are simply opening up the door to trouble. So do make sure that you keep in mind the fundamentals that have made you successful in the first place.

- **Anger.** This is another emotion that is hard to keep in check. When you get upset over anything, you might be tempted to act out irrationally. Simply put, if you are angry or upset over any unsatisfactory issues, then you might be better off simply sitting out a few rounds until you calm down. Believe it or not, hasty decisions can end up killing any progress you have made.

- **Desperation.** Unfortunately, some investors get into the FOREX market out of sheer desperation. They are in a dire financial situation. This leads them to pin their hopes on investment opportunities like FOREX to save the day. This can then lead to unrealistic expectations. When these folks see that money doesn't just fly out of the computer screen, they become increasingly desperate to make returns happen. This is where such folks are willing to take on unnecessary risk. They may be perfectly willing to go all-in hoping to hit a home run. In the end, they may very well hit that home run. But along the way, who knows what can happen.

The best way to offset this type of mentality is to maintain reasonable expectations. Sure, we all dream of scoring a huge hit that can suddenly make us wealthy, the fact of the matter is that the likelihood of such deals happening is once in a lifetime. So, setting up realistic expectations will help you keep your mind in check.

To set realistic expectations, think about the average return in the FOREX market. This is generally around 6% to 8%. When you look at the grander scheme of things, that's a pretty solid return. For the sake of simplicity, let's say that you earn 5% on average on every successful trade. That's money that can quickly add up.

Naturally, this type of return won't make you a millionaire overnight. But if you are prepared to be patient, you can earn a decent income out of trading. This is the best means of supplementing your income. Again, you might not become an overnight millionaire, but you'll at least put yourself in an incredible position down the road.

Another important aspect to keep in mind when managing your mindset is to have a clear goal in mind. If you are thinking, "I want to quit my job by the end of the year," you might be aiming a bit too high. However, if your plans are to put an extra couple of hundred bucks at the end of the month, then you have set yourself an attainable goal.

Let's consider how you can set a realistic goal in this regard: you start off with $500. Now, let's assume that you place 10 trades in a day. Let's go with the law of averages, so let's say that you'll win 5 trades and lose 5. This puts you at a 50% effectiveness rate. If you invest 2% of your investment capital in these 10 trades, you are investing a total of $100. At a 5% profit rate, you are making $5. If you keep your losses to a 5% average, you would break even.

The previous example may not seem particularly overwhelming. But if we upped the winning percentage to say 7 out of 10, then you are making the same 5%. However, you would only be losing about $2. All of a sudden, you have made a profit of $3.

For the sake of simplicity, this example highlights how you can make modest but solid returns. If we were to multiply these returns over a larger number of trades, you could potentially multiply $3 a hundred times over. This is where you begin to see solid returns.

Please note that making money on FOREX is a numbers game. As a result, the more successful trades you make, the more money you stand to earn. This differs greatly from trading stocks. In stock, you can hold on to a stock for months and clean up when the stock shoots through the roof. In FOREX, the longer you hold on to a position, the greater the likelihood you'll lose money. Hence, it's always best to liquidate your position as soon as you hit your take-profit point.

Don't Quit Your Day Job

One of the biggest motivators driving investors to get into the FOREX market is to achieve financial independence. This is certainly a reasonable goal to have. However, if you have your heart set on quitting your day job to become a full-time investor, then there is something you should know.

Full-time investors essentially trade their day job to spend the bulk of their productive hours pouring over charts and data. This means that you really need to be engaged with the prospect of investing in order to make this a career basically. If you only have a passing interest in FOREX, then it might be best for you to reconsider leaving your current employment.

When thinking about setting realistic expectations for your investment strategy, considering your FOREX endeavors as a means of supplementing your income is ideal. When you look at investments like FOREX as a means of giving you the extra income you need to pay debts and set yourself on the right track for financial freedom, you give yourself the breathing room you need.

In addition, when thinking about financial freedom, you are looking for the most important thing that we all search for: free time. Yes, financial freedom allows you to do with your time what you wish. This implies that having a steady stream of additional income will enable you to eventually take ownership of your time. Consequently, you won't have to be in the rat race your entire life. You will be able to make the most of your time with your family or any other activity you wish to engage in.

Another important consideration when it comes to investing is generating what is known as passive income. The term "passive income" means that you have income that you don't "work" for. Now, most folks confuse passive income with getting money for nothing. Please be advised that there is no such thing.

To generate passive income, you generally have to work a lot upfront before letting the source of income sit. Meanwhile, it is generating income for you while you only maintain it. This is the definition of passive income. When you work hard at learning FOREX, you will be able to generate enough trading strategies which can generate a steady income for you. As such, all you have to do is set them up and let them do the work for you.

That's all it takes.

Before you know it, you'll be making a decent living. On top of that, if you live a rather frugal lifestyle, you'll be sitting comfortably far sooner than you could have ever imagined.

Lastly, FOREX investing enables you to set up multiple income streams.

One of the pillars of financial independence is having multiple income streams. This term refers to setting up multiple sources of income that you can tap into throughout the month. This enables you to gain true independence as you don't

depend on just one source of income.

This is what allows you to achieve true freedom.

You see, when you don't depend on a single source of income, you are not overly concerned about what may happen if you lose one income stream. Should the worst happen, you can go on a replace a lost stream. However, when you depend on just one source of income, any sudden loss of that source will most likely destroy your finances. This is why having multiple sources is the most important thing you can do to ensure that you are on the right track.

Additionally, FOREX trading is the type of activity that you can integrate into your regular routine. This implies that you can easily incorporate your FOREX trading activities into your schedule. Sure, that might mean spending some time in the evenings or weekends at your computer. But please bear in mind that its part of that upfront effort that will end up paying off in the end. By the time you have achieved true mastery of the FOREX market, you'll be able to make trades easily and without much hassle.

Of course, there is one thing to consider though: never take your eye off the ball. So, even if you fully automate your trades, it's still important to make sure that you don't completely disconnect. By keeping tabs on the market, you can be sure that you will be able to handle any situation which may arise.

Maintaining a Healthy Body and Mind

An often-overlooked part of being a successful investor is staying healthy. It might not seem like it on the surface, but when you really think about it, it's important to balance every aspect of your life. Generally speaking, it's important to maintain a healthy mind-body connection. This is what helps you to focus and make the most of your energy.

When you are stressed out, tired and in a bad mood, you can't marshal your concentration to the point where you can really get the most out of your trading activity. For instance, if you are conducting research, you may not be able to focus enough attention on the charts and numbers you need to track. This may cause you to place trades in a haphazard fashion. Needless to say, this won't yield the best possible results.

Aside from the usual recommendations like eating healthy, getting exercise, and keeping stress at bay, it's worth noting that part of any successful trading plan involves taking care of your emotional wellbeing. On the whole, investing can get to be a bit stressful. While this doesn't mean that you will lose your hair from trading FOREX, the action can get a bit hot and heavy at times. For example, when you are under pressure after successive losses, you might feel compelled to make risky trades. Additionally, you may feel under intense pressure to make up your losses. While no one likes to lose, it's important to take losses in stride as much as you can. Losses are a part of life and should, therefore, be treated as such.

Another common issue with investors (this is very common among day traders) is that they tend to obsess with research. If you get caught up in the rigors of trading, you may end up becoming overly obsessed with conducting research and trading. As such, you might end up spending more time at your terminal than you should. This can lead to unhealthy habits, such as sitting down for too long. Also, it can take its toll on your mind, as trading is a very mental activity.

This is why successful investors look at FOREX as just another activity in their day. They set up routines and try to follow them as much as possible. They try to set a schedule that they know works for them. They also cap off their time at the terminal in order to avoid too much time in front of a screen. In doing this, they can refresh their mind and come back with more focus.

In particular, when you feel overwhelmed by too much data and information, taking time away can help you process the information that you have taken in. This is why playing sports, or engaging in any kind of physical activity, can help you clear your mind. When you do this, you are able to bounce back with more focus and energy. The last thing you want to do is put yourself in a position in which you are trudging along. If anything, trading FOREX is something which you should enjoy. Hence, forcing yourself to do it will never be conducive to obtaining successful results. So, do make an allowance for rest. Take care of your emotional and mental energy. You'll find that things get a lot easier that way.

CHAPTER 9

Most Popular Currencies In The Forex Market

By definition, trading FOREX is all about working with the world's entire currency supply. There are some currencies that are staples of the currency world, such as the US Dollar, the British Pound Sterling, the Japanese Yen, the Euro, and the Swiss Franc. Then, there are other important currencies such as the Canadian and Australian Dollar, Chinese Yuan, or the Mexican Peso.

All of these currencies are freely traded on the FOREX market, meaning that you can buy and sell them according to market prices and available supply. Consequently, you have every opportunity to make as much profit as you can based on your trades.

In the end, making a profit hinges on understanding the dynamics of the various currencies and the interactions. This largely depends on the relationships among countries and the frequency with which these currencies are traded together. Then, there are currencies that aren't usually traded together. In such cases, you need to be a bit more creative. Nevertheless, you can trade any currency at any time. It's up to you to do your homework on the best pairings that suit your particular investment strategy.

For example, if you choose to play it safe, then sticking to major currencies is your safest bet. If you are keen on making potentially significant gains, then you might try a road less traveled. This implies trading currencies which may not necessarily be commonly paired. It all boils down to the main objective you have in mind.

However, there is a word of caution here: for the novice investor, it's best to stick with more common currency pairings. As you gain more experience, you can venture out to other currencies. The important thing is to avoid taking on unnecessary risk at this point in the ballgame.

Major Currency Pairings

In the FOREX market, you'll find that certain currency pairs dominate the pace of the game. These pairs are called "correlated pairs" as they are commonly traded. Therefore, there is enough information to note that they move in accordance with the price action of each other. When one of the currencies has a significant shift, it directly impacts the other.

This is why understanding the nature of these pairings will enable you to make consistent profits. They may not be overwhelming, but they'll keep the lights on to be sure.

Here are the major currency pairs in the FOREX market today:

- The EUR/USD pair is the most commonly traded pair on the FOREX market. It accounts for roughly 20% of all transactions. For novice investors, this is the safest place to start. Here, you can find predictable results that will help you make money right from the start. You can copy-cat trades, too. That makes getting started even easier.

- The USD/JPY is generally regarded as the second-most traded pair. However, it does not account for nearly as much of the trading volume as the USD/EUR pair.

- The GBP/USD is also regarded as the third-place pair. This pair is generally traded on the European side of the market. Most American investors prefer the Euro.

- The USD/CHF pair is commonly traded as well though it does not account for nearly as much of the market share as some of the other pairs.

- Other interesting pairs include the USD/CAD, AUD/USD, and the NZD/USD. The NZD/AUD is also another correlated pair though its market share isn't nearly as significant as some of the other pairs on this list.

When you are first starting out in the FOREX market, it's best to stay with the major currency pairs. As we have mentioned earlier, you can get more creative as you gain more experience in the market. That is certainly valid as some unexpected pairings can provide you with the possibility of ample gains.

However, it's always best to do your research on these pairs before you take the plunge. While there is a good chance you'll clean up, there's also a good chance you'll fall short. So, do your homework before taking the plunge.

Determining the Price of Major Currency Pairs

The main reason why we recommend novice investors to deal with major currency is pairs is simple: volume. These are the currencies that attract the largest amount of transactions. As a result, novice investors can expect more bang for their buck, so to speak.

When there is a greater deal of trading volume, there is a greater chance for the strategies that we have highlighted throughout this book to work. When there is a smaller trading volume, the strategies which we have presented herein may not hold up quite as well. This is why dealing with lesser-known currencies should be done under very strict supervision.

That being said, the price of major currency pairs is set by supply and demand. This is why a large trading volume tends to minimize significant shifts in the price of major pairs. On the contrary, currencies that don't have a large trading volume may suffer significant shifts from a single trade. This can ultimately ruin your chances of making a profit.

With large, institutional investors, the kind that have positions in the millions of dollars, they tend to choose major currencies over lesser-known ones because the supply is large enough to hold such large trading positions. So, smaller investors can ride the coattails of large investors. When you trade along with the big firms, you can ride the top of the wave. This may not yield you millions of dollars, but it is certainly a great way of making a healthy profit.

For example, the EUR/USD rate sits at 1.10. This means that the cost of 1 Euro is $1.10. If the price suddenly moves to 1.12, it means that the Euro has gained value against the dollar as it costs more dollars to purchase a Euro. However, if the price drops to $1.08, then the dollar has gained value as it costs fewer dollars to purchase one Euro. Depending and what you're banking on, you can come out on top. The main thing to keep in mind is that the various factors in the market will ultimately determine the behavior of the price action among the major pairs. So, always be on the lookout.

Investing in Cryptocurrency

In recent years, cryptocurrencies, or cryptos, have become quite popular, especially after the meteoric rise of Bitcoin. The wild ride that saw Bitcoin soar to over $20,000 per coin landed cryptos on everyone's radar. Given the massive upside of cryptos, practically anyone that could get into the crypto market did. Unfortunately, some got hammered when the price of Bitcoin fell back down to Earth. Nevertheless, Bitcoin is not the only game in town.

Yet, cryptos are not widely understood by the average investor. That's why we are going to go over what cryptos are and how you can make money on from trading in cryptos. Additionally, you will find that cryptos are still in their infancy. This means that there is a massive upside which you can exploit.

It is important to underscore the fact that cryptos are not money in the traditional sense. A cryptocurrency is a type of digital token that can be used to settle transactions, among other uses. For instance, is one individual sells a car to another, the deal can be settled by exchanging digital tokens as opposed to using traditional currency. This is what makes cryptocurrencies so interesting to the average investor.

When you deal with cryptos, you are essentially dealing with 1s and 0s. These can be used for identification purposes, keeping track of volume, and even to facilitate government actions. Indeed, there are many types of uses for cryptos.

At this point, the expression of cryptos' value is seen in traditional currencies such as US Dollars. In this case, you can purchase cryptos by exchanging US Dollars (or any other accepted currency). The digital tokens are stored in a virtual wallet or vault. This vault contains the codes that lead to the access of your coins. You can then trade them to other users in exchange for other tokens, or traditional currency.

It should also be noted that cryptos don't trade like currencies do on the FOREX market. They trade more like commodities. A good example we can use to compare the value of cryptos is oil. Oil is a commodity and is traded at spot price. Spot price means the current price of the commodity at the time the trade is placed. Consequently, the same market forces apply here. Supply and demand are what drive the valuation of all cryptos. Some have an enormous issuance, such as millions of coins. Depending on their popularity, investors may choose to pay an increasingly higher value for them.

Trading Cryptocurrencies

Cryptos are not traded on the open market. This means that you need to go through a crypto exchange. These exchanges work in the same manner as FOREX does. The difference lies in that you are not trading "real" currencies. Rather, you are exclusively dealing with cryptos.

In a crypto exchange, you can use US Dollars, for instance, to purchase coins. You can then sell them back to other users for a profit or loss, depending on the outcome of the trade. Alternatively, you can choose to hold on to them as long as you wish. The main thing here is to be cognizant of the price.

Since price fluctuates freely, you need to pay attention to the quotes for standard cryptos. Thus, you can track their value and sell whenever you like. One thing to note here is that crypto trading is much simpler than FOREX. You don't need quite the complicated setup to trade cryptos. All you need is to buy and then sell. However, you need to keep your eye on the ball.

The good side of this is that cryptos don't have nearly the same trading volume as FOREX does. So, you shouldn't expect a second-by-second price action. You can determine the price action over much longer timeframes such as hours or even days. If you are proficient in chart reading, you can easily detect patterns in charts. Thus, you won't have to spend hours reading technical data.

Best Cryptos to Trade

This is a question that is commonly posed. For most folks, cryptos equal Bitcoin. As we have mentioned, Bitcoin is not the only game in town.

So, here are the top 10 cryptos you can trade today based on their market cap:

1. Bitcoin
2. Ethereum
3. XRP
4. Tether
5. Bitcoin Cash
6. Bitcoin SV
7. Litecoin
8. EOS
9. Binance Coin
10. Tezos

While this list is hardly exhaustive (there are over 5,000 cryptos in the market today), these offer the best chance for you to make some returns when trading. You can go on a crypto exchange like Coinbase to learn more about how you can open an account. Then, you can begin trading in these coins. The best thing about this list is that they all have varying prices. So, you don't have to shell out $10,000 for one Bitcoin. In fact, some trade for a little as a few pennies on the Dollar. As such, there is a price for everyone.

While there are other exchanges out there, the main thing to keep in mind is that the same rules apply. It's important to focus on reputable companies that offer a solid reputation and a good track record. Additionally, you will find that reputable crypto trade exchanges offer a great deal of support. After all, they are interested in facilitating trade as much as possible so that others can join. Consequently, you can expect to get a great deal of help when starting out trading cryptos.

CONCLUSION

Thank you very much for making it all the way to the end of this book. It has been quite a trip as we have covered a lot of information. We have gone over FOREX and how you can use this market to your full advantage.

So, the time has come for you to get started on the journey that is trading FOREX. At the outset of this book, we asked you not to begin trading until you made it all the way to the end. As such, we hope that you now feel confident in taking the plunge. While it might seem a bit daunting, don't worry. Every investor that starts out in this market often feels overwhelmed. The great thing is that you now have all of the tools you need to get started.

Please make the time to further your study of the FOREX market. It's imperative that you focus on improving your skills as much as possible. When you are committed to improving your skills, you will find that it's not nearly as hard as you might have thought. The only requirement here is to focus your concentration on making sense of the currency pairings you are studying. In this regard, going over charts, numbers, and technical data is essential in gaining the experience you need to become a great trader.

Also, please make sure that you follow the guidelines which we have outlined pertaining to choosing the right broker. In doing so, you will have made one of the most important decisions of your life. By choosing the right broker, you'll be able to give yourself the biggest advantage you could.

Now, please take the time to go over any parts of this book that you would like to dig deeper into. Do take the time to drill down as much as you can in any of the parts of this book. You will find that repetition is the best way to deepen learning. Moreover, you will always discover new things every time you read this book.

Furthermore, take full advantage of the free demo time reputable trading platforms provide. This time is highly useful in learning the ropes of FOREX trading without betting the farm. By the time you are ready to go live, you'll be confident in making the right types of deals. All you need is some time and practice to get up to speed.

So, thank you once again for taking the time to read this book. If you have found it to be useful, in any way, please tell your friends, family, colleagues, and associates about it. We are sure that they will also find it insightful. In particular, anyone who is looking to learn more about the exciting world of FOREX trading will surely find this book to be a great starting point.

The time has come to make some real money trading FOREX. What are you waiting for? Got get'em!

Forex and Cryptocurrency

The Ultimate Guide to Trading Forex and Cryptos. How to Make Money Online By Trading Forex and Cryptos in 2020.

DAVID UCHIHA

INTRODUCTION

Welcome to *Forex and Cryptocurrency The Ultimate Guide to Trading Forex and Cryptos. How to Make Money Online By Trading Forex and Cryptos in 2020.* If you are reading this, you will find a trove of information that will help you to make sound investment decisions in the world of FOREX and cryptocurrencies.

This book is intended for all newcomers to both the world of FOREX and cryptos. We will be discussing the fundamentals of both of these markets in great detail. The main objective is to provide you with an education in this subject so that you can make sound investment decisions leading you to maximize your profits and obtain the best possible returns for your investment dollars.

Unlike the stock market, the FOREX and cryptos markets are open 24 hours a day. This means that you can trade any time you wish. This opens up a number of interesting possibilities as you can invest in both FOREX and cryptos without having to quit your day job or significantly alter your regular routine. In fact, all you need to do is make sure that you have the right setup to get started.

That's why we're here... we're here because we want to give you a head start that we wish we could have had when starting out investing. You see, most investors become successful through trial and error. Many times, you have to lose a great deal of money before you can become rich. Unfortunately, some investors lose their shirts before they can make serious money.

That doesn't have to be your case. With the education you will get in this book, you'll be able to make money without having to lose your shirt in the process. If anything, you'll have to become a student of these markets. After all, all successful investors dedicate time and attention to the study of their chosen market. Such investors strive to learn as much as they can. In doing so, they are able to maximize their returns without having to sacrifice their capital in the process.

If you are brand new to investing, don't worry. We have you covered. You don't need an advanced degree in finance to cash in on the markets. All you need is the willingness to put in the time and effort needed to learn the way the FOREX and crypto markets work. Once you get started, you'll see that these markets are not quite as complex as you might have thought. Sure, they do have their intricacies. But then again, with the education you can expect here, you won't be second-guessing.

So, let's get started on the journey that will lead you to become financially independent. At the end of the day, that's what all great investors seek. They are all after making as much money as they can so that their families are provided for. In addition, making money isn't so much a question of greed; it's a question of earning enough money to ensure security. This kind of security comes by way of financial independence.

Let's get on with it!

CHAPTER 1

Introduction To Forex And Cryptocurrency Trading

FOREX and cryptocurrencies (also known as "cryptos") are financial markets in which investors come together to make deals for the purpose of earning a profit. This is important to note as investors are not in it to lose money. They are in it to make as much money as possible. Naturally, there are winners and losers. Nevertheless, all investors try to be on the winning end as much as possible.

On the whole, most folks tend to become confused by the various types of financial markets. For instance, stocks are an entirely different market. There are also bonds, commodities, and derivatives. All of these markets have their characteristics. If you are keen on learning about them, by all means, take the time to do the research you need.

As for the FOREX market, you will find that it is the most dynamic of all financial markets. The reason for this is that FOREX is the most liquid market in the world. Since you are essentially trading currency, you are swapping money for money. This is something that you can do right from the comfort of your home. Best of all, FOREX is a 24-hour market as you are trading currency from all over the world. In short, you can trade anytime and anywhere.

This is why FOREX is so attractive to investors around the world.

However, FOREX is not for the faint of heart. FOREX requires you to pay close attention to the dynamics of the market itself. This means that you need to study what's happening so that you can be ready for any changes which may emerge. You can profit greatly from these changes, or you can sustain significant losses. It's all in the way you manage the situation unfolding around you.

Types of FOREX Markets

Considering that the FOREX market is essentially a marketplace in which currency is bought and sold, it behaves just like any other market. This implies that the great equalizer of the FOREX market is price. The difference here lies in the fact that price does not reflect the valuation of a commodity such as a car, a house, or a pair of jeans. In this case, price is the reflection of the valuation of one currency versus another. What this means is that you understand the value of one currency as it is expressed in terms of another.

The same situation occurs with any other commodity on the planet. The difference lies in the fact that it's easier to grasp the concept of a pair of jeans costing X amount of dollars as opposed to one Euro costing X amount of dollars.

With that in mind, FOREX is all about finding the mechanisms in which you can take one sum of money, exchanging it for another, and then exchanging that currency back into the original currency, for a profit, of course. This is the basic mechanism that you can use to conduct FOREX trades.

Just like other financial markets, there are several types of markets within the FOREX domain. So, we're going to be taking a look at what they are their characteristics.

The Spot Market

This type of market receives its name as it deals with the trade of currency at current prices. The current price of a currency is reflected by its exchange rate. In essence, an exchange rate is the ratio of one currency in terms of another.

When you travel, you commonly see exchange rates at airports. For instance, if you exchange US Dollars into Mexican Pesos, you might find that you'll get twenty-some Pesos for one US Dollar. This is an exchange rate. It is the price that a person is willing to pay or receive for another currency.

Also, you'll find the term "cross rates." While exchange and cross rates tend to be used synonymously, the difference lies in that exchange rates are used for the purpose of converting currency. The term cross rate is generally used as a reference regarding the valuation of one currency in terms of another. Additionally, you'll also find that leading currencies are "quoted" in terms of various currencies. This serves as a reference for investors who deal in international business.

As such, the spot market is where you buy and sell currency at current market prices. Market prices are set by supply and demand. These market forces converge as holders of currency look to sell while buyers look to find supply. In a perfect equilibrium, that is, there is a balance between buyers and sellers, price tends to be stable. This means that there is very little shift in price, if any. When there is an imbalance in market forces, the price tends to fluctuate accordingly. Generally speaking, when there is a greater supply, price tends to fall. When there is a greater demand, price tends to rise.

However, these market forces are immutable and may be subject to changes depending on the overall conditions of the market itself.

The most straightforward way to make money on FOREX is to buy low and sell high. However, this isn't always the case. In FOREX, there are times when you can make money by falling price. It all depends on what your objectives are.

The Futures Market

Since price (exchange rates) are set by market forces, you are subject to the fluctuations in price. This means that there is nothing you can really do to prevent prices from moving, or to influence them in the direction you wish. Unless you hold a vast investment capital, or if your influence is great on investor psyche, then you are basically at the mercy of market forces.

Often, both businessmen and investors look to reduce their exposure to this type of risk by engaging in the futures market. As its name suggests, you are making deals for the future. As such, this implies that you make a deal today with hopes of reducing your exposure to risk in the future.

For instance, you wish to purchase Swiss Francs in a month's time. However, you are concerned about the exchange rate down the road. So, you can take out a futures contract so that you lock in today's exchange rate on a deal that will happen in a month's time. Your counterpart will engage in the deal while also charging you a commission for their trouble. Often, the commission (also known as a "premium") you pay for the contract itself is far less than the difference you might have to pay if you don't take out the contract.

Some contracts stipulate that you don't have to execute the deal if you don't want to. In this case, you have an option to go through with the contract or not. If you choose not to go through with the deal, then all you lose is the premium you paid for the issuance of the contract.

As for international business, taking out these types of contracts makes a great deal of sense as it allows them to get a handle on their costs. This enables companies to reduce the risk of having raw materials, supplies, or merchandise skyrocket unexpectedly due to fluctuations in exchange rates. Also, it secures them funds that they can use to make payments. As a result, the futures market is a very active market in which you can engage if you choose to do so.

The Forward Market

On the whole, the forward market is the same as the futures market. The forward market is characterized by locking in current prices for a future deal. The difference lies in that the entire set of conditions surrounding these contracts are completely customizable. As a result, you can configure them to suit your individual needs and conditions.

In the forward market, it's common to find "options contracts." These contracts contain the various conditions which we have already described with the particular difference that they give holders an option to buy, or sell, depending on the specific terms of the deal. This implies that if holders are not keen on enacting the contract itself, they can choose not to go through with it. In the end, they only lose the underwriting fee charge for the contract.

The forward market can be a good source of deals for you. So, do look into it should you be interested in making the most of the potential deals in this type of market. Ultimately, you will have the choice to go through with the contract if it is best for you at that specific point in time.

Forex and Cryptocurrency

For most folks, understanding what cryptocurrency is can be challenging. On the whole, a crypto functions just like a regular currency. However, the difference lies in that crypto is a fully digital currency. This means that it will never have any physical issuance, as is the case of regular government-issued currencies.

In this case, cryptos are used in a digital sphere meaning that they are used solely within digital transactions. This implies that you would never be able to use crypto in a cash transaction, as is the case many times. For example, you could barter the sale of an item at a garage sale. But the payment for the item would happen digitally. As such, no cash would exchange hands.

Beyond that main difference, cryptos trade exactly the same way as a regular currency would. This is why investors are keen on cryptos as they function much the same way money does. Additionally, they can also be traded in the same manner that regular currencies are traded.

The reason why cryptocurrencies were born is due to the slowness that governments have had in reacting to the increasing presence of the digital world. Since there is a great deal of business taking place digitally, digital platforms and payment systems are needed. However, it's not always easy to transition from regular hard currencies to a digital system. This implies a need for banks to adapt their practices to suit the needs of online business.

To solve this, cryptocurrencies emerged. In addition, cryptocurrencies are meant to be used as a means of avoiding the traditional banking system. While the intent is not to circumvent traditional banking for the purpose of illegal activity (though cryptos are the currency of choice for criminal groups), the fact of the matter is that using cryptos facilitates a great deal of transactions.

In fact, one of the core tents of cryptos is to facilitate transparency. Given the social nature of cryptos, users are put into a position in which they must ensure transparency at various turns. This is due to the shared ledger technology of the blockchain. In addition, transactions can't be simply erased from the system. Since there are multiple entries at various points in the system, erasing a transaction is impossible. This means that all transactions conducted in a specific cryptocurrency are recorded forever. This fosters transparency at all turns.

Top Cryptocurrencies

When talking about cryptos, it's safe to assume that the top one that comes to mind is Bitcoin. Since Bitcoin arrived on the scene in 2009, it exploded in popularity until it became the most-traded asset in recent history. In fact, the craze for Bitcoin got to be so big that it soared to over $20,000 per coin. If only individual stocks or commodities could reach these heights.

The reason why Bitcoin reached this price point is due to its relative scarcity. You see, Bitcoin is quite hard to produce. Given the nature of the blockchain and the computing power it takes to solve the math problems behind each transaction, individual Bitcoins have become quite hard to produce. Since there is a finite supply of Bitcoins, investors and speculators decided to get in on the action.

However, like all financial assets, the market could only take so much.

Eventually, Bitcoin's market valuation fell from $20,000 a coin to about $3,000 before rebounding to about $10,000. These wild swings are relatively common with newer assets, particularly when investors flock to enter the market on the fear of missing out. And while there has been talk of market manipulation, the fact remains that Bitcoin is the leader in the crypto space by far.

But it should also be noted that Bitcoin is not the only show in town. There are hundreds of other cryptos out there. Most of them don't sell for very much. In fact, you can get some for a little as pennies on the Dollar. Then, there are others which trade for considerably more.

Here is a list of the top 10 cryptos on the market today based on the market cap.

1. Bitcoin (BTC) $128bn

2. Ethereum (ETH) $19.4bn

3. XRP (XRP) $8.22bn

4. Tether (USDT) $6.4bn

5. Bitcoin Cash (BCH) $4.1bn

6. Bitcoin SV (BSV) $3.4bn

7. Litecoin (LTC) $2.6bn

8. EOS (EOS) $2.4bn

9. Binance Coin (BNB) $2.4bn

10. Tezos (XTZ) $1.5bn

There are some familiar names on this list, and some not-so. This list includes major players like Bitcoin, Ethereum, and Litecoin. Some not-so-familiar names include XRP and Tezos. Nevertheless, these coins have a considerable market cap. These are the market values estimated for the total amount of coins in existence for each crypto multiplied by their value per coin.

As you can see, there is a considerable amount of money in play within the crypto market. In total, there are 5,392 total cryptocurrencies (as of April 2020) with a total market value of $201bn.

That's a nice chunk of change.

What's more, cryptos are traded just like any other currency on the market today. This means that you have the unique opportunity to take part in a $200-billion market. Hence, there is a lot of money to be made by savvy investors.

One more thing: technology is the future now as it has always been. Therefore, the use of cryptos for everyday use will soon become a reality. That's why it's best to get in on the ground floor now, build up your portfolio and move on from there. You will surely find that the value there is to be made in this market will entice you to dig deeper into the possibility of investing and making a healthy profit.

Basic Forex Terminology

Like any other discipline, FOREX has a set of specialized vocabulary which you need to become familiar with. So, here are the main terms which you will find throughout this book.

Cryptocurrency. A digital currency that has many of the same functions as a regular fiat-based currency. It is digital in nature and contains specific encryption mechanisms that are used to regulate its issuance and use. These methods are used to verify the transfer of funds and operate independently of any country's jurisdiction. They are backed by the confidence of users and can be found on specific platforms created for their use.

Currency. The official government-issued means of payment which enables users to buy and sell goods and services. Currency acts as money as it is a store of wealth and allows for the measurement of the value of goods. It is also a means of settling accounts while also enabling individuals to transact across countries. Currency is issued by a central bank and backed by the financial position of a government.

Exchange rate. The expression of the value of one currency in terms of another. Exchange rates are the ratio in which one currency can be converted into another. For the purpose of international business transactions, various currencies may be used. Therefore, an exchange rate serves to create a means of establishing parameters of comparison among various currencies. Exchange rates also serve as a pricing mechanism in which foreign exchange markets can price one currency in relation to another.

FOREX. This is the "foreign exchange" market. It is the marketplace in which buyers and sellers of currency meet. Nowadays, it is a digital marketplace where transactions occur over the internet. Payments and accounts are settled electronically. The physical location of the FOREX market is the New York Stock Exchange in New York. However, virtually all of the transactions on the FOREX market happen over a digital platform. Investors who gain access to this platform can conduct trades without the need to be physically present at the stock exchange.

Leverage. This refers to the amount of funds needed to place a trade. In a manner of speaking, leverage means that you can place trades whose value is greater than the amount of funds you have deposited in your account. When you are required to have full backing, you cannot place a trade beyond the amount of money you have deposited in your account. However, if you are not required to have any amount of money deposited, you essentially have 100% leveraging. At 50% leverage, you can place a $100 trade with $50 deposited in your account.

Margin. Margin refers to the difference between the money you have deposited in your account and the value of your trade. If you place a trade using leverage, you will earn a margin when you make a profit. If you lose money on the trade, then you need to cover that margin. In such cases, you may get a "margin call." This means that the brokerage firm you are working with will ask you to pay the difference for the loss you have incurred. If your account has sufficient funds, the fund will simply be deducted.

PIP. "Price in points" or, pip, is the individual measure for the profit or loss in FOREX. Generally speaking, pips refer to percentage points on a trade. Pips are relative to the specific cross rates of two currencies. This means that if you have a 1:1 cross rate, pips will represent a much higher value than if you had a 1:100 cross rate.

Profit/loss. Simply put, this the money you make, or lose, on each trade. In FOREX, the stop-loss point refers to the point where you cut your losses, and the take-profit point alludes to the point in which you will exit a trade with the profit you have indicated.

Resistance level. This is the highest point in a data series, meaning the highest price point that a currency pair will hit before coming back down. The "resistance" is created as the price does not move beyond this point. When price pushes past a resistance level, the term "breakout" is used to refer to this situation.

Spread. Spread is the difference between your stop-loss and take-profit points. Essentially, you measure the difference between the amount of money you expect to make and the largest loss you are prepared to take.

Support level. This level refers to the lowest price point in a data set. This point serves as "support" as the price does not move below it. The main reason for this is that investors jump in to purchase at this point, thereby raising the price back up to the eventual resistance level. When prices fall through the support level, this is referred to as a "breakthrough."

CHAPTER 2

Fundamentals Of Cryptocurrency And The Blockchain

It seems that "cryptocurrency" and the "blockchain" have become buzzwords in recent years. Anyone who is looking into becoming an investor seems to be interested in getting a piece of the action. Since you are reading this book, it's fair to say you too, are interested in getting a piece of the action. As such, we will be looking at the fundamentals of cryptocurrency and the blockchain so that you can gain a much better perspective on this matter. In addition, we'll be discussing the overall functioning of this technology and what it means to the average individual.

It should be noted that the concept of cryptocurrency was born out of the need to have a means of payment that could go outside of the usual government-controlled systems. The idea was to create a safe and secure means of creating transactions in such a way that users could be certain that each transaction is fully secured.

This is important to note as most transactions, digital or otherwise, don't always have a secure platform. In fact, regular transactions lend themselves to fraud and illegal activity. In particular, cash economies create vast underground networks that criminals can exploit. Thoughts of drug dealers exchanging suitcases full of cash come to mind.

Consequently, cryptos are meant to work outside of usual central bank control while ensuring full transparency for all users. Nevertheless, critics of cryptos have pointed to the fact that criminals use cryptos to engage in financial transactions as these digital currencies work outside of networks supervised by law enforcement agencies.

This is true of lesser-known crypto. As a matter of fact, some cryptos have been created for this specific purpose. But when you deal with "official" cryptos, that is digital currencies that are fully transparent by the entire internet, so to speak, you know you have the assurance that you are not dealing with criminals. Rather, you are dealing with other folks who want a secure means of conducting business.

What Is the Blockchain?

When digital currencies first arrived on the scene, the concept of blockchain was born. Since then, this term has been replaced with the term "digital ledger." The reason for this name is that the blockchain is exactly that, a digital ledger.

If we consider traditional accounting principles, double-entry bookkeeping has a party and a counterparty in every register. Therefore, the blockchain uses this system to keep track of transactions. However, it takes this concept one step further by adding a third party who is in charge of verifying every transaction. In a manner of speaking, it's like having two friends agree on a bet and then having a third friend witness the agreement.

In this exact manner, the blockchain is able to ensure that every transaction is fully transparent. In order to conduct a transaction, both parties must be registered and verified users. This means that there are no anonymous individuals who can pretend to be someone else. If you are not verified, you cannot deal with official cryptos.

Furthermore, the third party, which certifies the transaction, must also be duly verified. This is what gives credence to the verification process. Once the transaction has been completed and verified, it is registered on multiple servers throughout the world. Thus, there is no centralization of data. If a user wished to erase a transaction, they would have to erase all servers on which the transaction was recorded. This is virtually impossible, as knowing the exact number of servers is quite difficult. Plus, all data can be quickly copied on to additional serves. As such, anyone wishing to erase transactions would need to shut the entire internet down, scour every possible server for records, and then delete them.

But then again, anyone with a copy on a hard drive that is not connected to the internet could simply upload them again.

Do you see why this system ensures full transparency?

The Verification Process

This is where the blockchain gets a bit tricky.

When a transaction between two parties takes place, it is not official until it has been verified by a third party. Once the third party has gotten on the blockchain to verify the process, the transaction is finalized, and the seller receives payment.

The way the verification process works is through the solution of a math problem. The third party that verifies the transaction must successfully solve a mathematical problem in order to successfully authenticate the deal. However, for this process to truly work, each problem has to be unique. Once a specific problem has been solved, it can never be used again. For instance, $2+2 = 4$ can only be used once. Upon its solution, it is registered so it can never be used again.

Given this specific characteristic, the blockchain needs to generate more and more problems in order to satisfy the amount of transactions. In theory, there is an infinite number of math problems to be solved. Consequently, there is potential for an unlimited number of transactions. Nevertheless, as transactions go, the difficulty of problems increases.

Now, it should be noted that these problems are not solved by hand; that is, the problem isn't solved by a person working with pen and paper. A computer would do that for them. The issue here is that the complexity of math problems consumes a certain amount of computing power.

This is where the challenge lies.

At first, the computing power needed to solve basic math problems was minuscule and could be completed in a matter of nanoseconds. However, the estimated amount of computing power needed to solve the blockchain's current problems is estimated to surpass the power of the average computer. Thus, an average computer needs several minutes to complete the verification problem. This is why the blockchain has slowed down in recent times.

By now, the blockchain is still functional. However, its future is rather unclear as there is no real way of predicting if it is sustainable indefinitely. Most experts agree that the blockchain is unsustainable as the amount of electricity that is required to run the verification process is quite large. Thus, other iterations of cryptos will eventually replace the blockchain with a much less energy-intensive system.

Coin Creation and Offering

At the outset of the blockchain, there wasn't a single coin in circulation. This meant that each coin had to be created by transactions that did not include a coin that was already in existence. Therefore, the two parties would make a deal, and after the verification process, they would be able to create a new coin.

The reason for this system was so that only the absolutely necessary number of coins would be created. This was purposely done to avoid the uncontrolled issuance of currency that governments engage in. As a result, only a set number of coins would be used to conduct a specific number of transactions.

Initially, it was thought that the blockchain could produce enough coins to run the entire world economy. However, experience has proven this to not be the case. There is a finite number of coins as the computing power and electricity needed to create them would eventually surpass humankind's ability. Thus, the only choice here would be to create a fixed number of coins.

The workaround to this situation was to create multiple cryptos in order to share the load, so to speak. Since then, a great deal of coins has been created. Some have quickly gained popularity, while others have remained within a niche market of users. For instance, gaming communities use very specific cryptos for in-app purchases or transactions during gameplay.

Other cryptos have taken the route that is known as an "initial coin offering" or ICO. An ICO is very similar to an IPO with a stock. In an ICO, the creator(s) of the crypto issues an initial number of coins which users can purchase at a specified market price. Like IPOs, underwriters determine the valuation of each coin based on its potential and possible utility. Some ICOs have been widely successful, while others have been a flop. Still, ICOs are generally met with the same expectation as IPOs, that is, the hope that an investor can get in early and clean up when the market begins to push up the price.

The History of the Blockchain

It might surprise you to find that the blockchain, at least the concept of it, dates back to the early 90s. Around that time, when the internet first began to emerge, so did the idea of a system in which computer networks could be used to conduct financial transactions. And so, the concept of the blockchain was born.

Since then, numerous attempts were made to bring this process to life. But it wasn't until computing power caught up to this idea that it became practical. That's why around 2008, Satoshi Nakamoto (pseudonym for the creator of Bitcoin) was able to make the blockchain operational. With the emergence of Bitcoin, literally, thousands of cryptos have come into existence. As such, we now have a myriad of coins to choose from.

But we need to go all the way back to 1991 to find that Stuart Haber and W Scott Stornetta first described the concept of what would become the blockchain. Their work revolutionized the information world though it was nothing more than a pipedream them.

In 1998, the first decentralized digital currency emerged as Nick Szabo began work on what was then known as "bit gold." The idea was to create the world's first digital currency, that is, a currency that wasn't controlled by a government or central bank.

A couple of years later, in 2000, Stefan Konst developed his theory on "cryptographic secured chains." These led to a set of guidelines on how they could be implemented for the purpose of ensuring that the idea of a decentralized currency could become a reality.

However, it wasn't until 2008 that developer(s) working under the guise of Satoshi Nakamoto published a white paper for the eventual model of what would become the blockchain as we know it today. It is unclear whether it was a single developer, or most likely a group of developers who published this paper.

By 2009, the first public ledger was made available for transactions by means of Bitcoin. This is the birth of the blockchain. It also led to the creation of the first lot of Bitcoins. It should be noted that they were practically worthless as the public was yet to catch on to its usefulness.

The blockchain 2.0 was developed in 2014. This enabled digital ledger technology to be implemented for transactions that went beyond financial dealings. For instance, it could be used for personal identification purposes or virtually any other type of purpose that users could consider useful.

Following the emergence of the second generation blockchain, other cryptos began to emerge. This is the case of Ethereum, Litecoin, and Ripple, among many others. In the case of Ripple, it resembles Bitcoin quite a bit though its technology makes it a lot easier to authenticate than Bitcoin. This is due to the fact that Ripple was created for the sole purpose of settling accounts, meaning facilitating transactions. It's based on a public ledger. As such, operations can be easily verified so that full transparency is ensured.

As for Ethereum, this is a separate blockchain that produces a coin called "ether." This technology allows for the creation of what are known as "smart contracts." In other words, contracts among individuals can be authenticated and enforced by means of this technology. Additionally, the Ethereum network can issue as many coins as needed without having to go through the creation process that Bitcoin has.

How Blockchain Changed Digital Money and Transactions

Considering the fact that the main purpose of the blockchain was to facilitate transactions and ensure transparency, it should be said that this type of technology has revolutionized the world. Consequently, there is a greater possibility of a decentralized financial system.

This is the underlying tenet of the blockchain and cryptocurrencies as the main purpose is to create a monetary system in which users could be free to conduct business without having to go through the supervision of a government and its monetary agencies.

Naturally, this is a revolutionary concept as governments have cracked down on activity that is outside of its jurisdiction. However, the internet is a truly vast domain in which a single institution is unable to regulate the entire number of transactions that take place.

Additionally, traditional fiat currency, even when it's used in digital format such as through e-banking, still has its limitation. For instance, it is practically impossible to issue new currency as needed, particularly when the volume of transactions picks up. This is a key factor that has limited the growth of business. And while governments can just issue as much currency as they want at a stroke of a pen, it's really not that easy. There are checks and balances that must be met in order for currency creation to take place.

Moreover, currency creation is not an act that reflects economic logic. Most of the time, monetary policy reflects political issues and considerations. As a result, monetary policy tends to be restrictive and works on a lag.

On the whole, the decentralization of currency makes it possible for individuals to conduct business freely. This implies that accounts and transactions can be settled publicly and transparently without having to limit the number of transactions.

Crypto's biggest detractors claim that cryptos lend themselves to corruption and crime. For example, terrorists can negotiate dealings by using cryptos. After all, they are anonymous as they don't require a passport for a transaction to be verified.

However, this has yet to be proven on a public ledger network. If anything, such shady transactions happen on the deep web. In this domain, there is literally no control or regulation. Nevertheless, the average citizen will never go anywhere near the dark web. So, it's safe to say that for now there is no shady business going on.

The main grievance that governments have with blockchain technology is that these transactions are not susceptible to taxation. This implies that accounts can be settled using cryptos without any proceeds going to the government in terms of taxation. This is why efforts are being made to find a means of taxing transactions made with cryptos. While there is no official ban on cryptos, most governments are reluctant to allow cryptos to be "legal," even though they are not breaking or circumventing any laws.

On the whole, the blockchain looks to become the wave of the future for business. As the world becomes more and more technologically inclined, cryptos, or digital currencies for that matter, will take over the vast majority of financial transactions. Perhaps there will still be a place for physical money. However, the outlook is that everyone on the planet will eventually have a digital wallet in which their wealth can be stored seemingly forever.

Private Vs. Public Blockchains

So far, we have talked about "the blockchain" as if there were only one in existence. However, you might be surprised to find that there are a number of blockchains in existence. Some are public such as is the case of Bitcoin, and some are private. Private blockchains are limited to a certain number of users. These users gain access through whatever means creators provide and can only transact within that blockchain using its corresponding cryptos.

This is important to note as a blockchain does not necessarily have to be open to the entire planet. The verification and authentication process can happen in a reduced group of people. The idea is that as long as everyone trusts everyone who's on the blockchain, then the blockchain serves its purpose.

The existence of private blockchains has led to the idea of countries creating their own national blockchains. These private blockchains would be limited to the citizens of a country with a national crypto in place. On the surface, this seems like a highly practical approach. However, the reality is that it would function pretty much the same as the current fiat-based currency system. And while there would be greater transparency, the fact of the matter is that the main objective of decentralization would not occur.

This is why the world strives for the implementation of truly global, public blockchains that can govern most of the transactions in the world. On the flip side, detractors claim that truly public blockchains would eliminate privacy. This is a valid consideration when you factor in that not everyone wants their purchases to be made public for the entire world to see. Perhaps it's not so much a question of trying to hide something. Still, the fact is that privacy is the biggest concern that stems from the implementation of truly public digital ledger technology.

Ultimately, there needs to be a balance. This is why having both public and private blockchains can allow users to have a greater sense of both transparency and privacy. Perhaps there needs to be levels in which transactions would be considered public while others would be considered private. These levels could be the result of consensus among citizens. However, it's important to understand that if left up to the government to regulate, the blockchain would become just as bureaucratic as the current financial system is.

In the end, digital currencies are still in their infancy. There are a number of issues that need to be worked out so that digital currencies can truly satisfy the needs of the market. Perhaps at some point down the road, this technology will be practical enough so that we can develop a truly decentralized monetary system which can provide every citizen of the world the opportunity to live on equal footing. For now, only time will tell. Yet, you have the opportunity to take advantage of the crypto space. After all, this is what this book is all about.

CHAPTER 3

Cryptocurrency Regulations

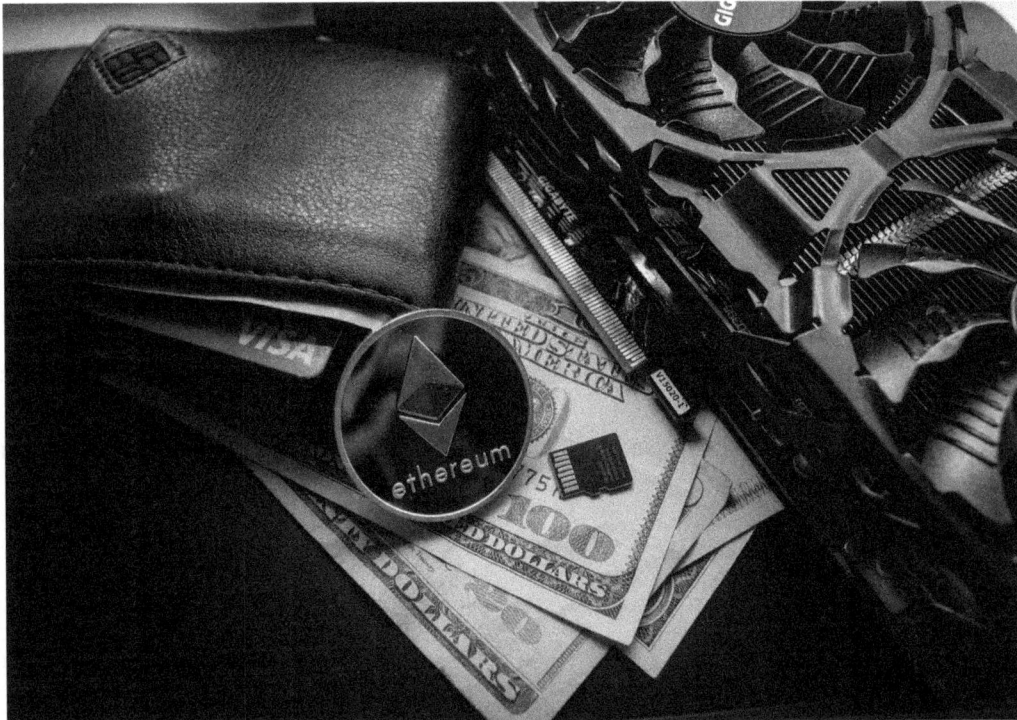

To understand the significance of cryptos, it's important to understand the nature of money and currency.

By definition, money serves as a medium of exchange. This implies that any commodity which is used as money must serve as a means of facilitating trade among all parties involved. Consequently, both buyers and sellers must agree that the commodity used to finalize a transaction is valid. For instance, if the two sides in the negotiation decided to use water as money, both sides must agree that water sufficiently represents the value that the commodity encompasses. As a result, the buyer is happy to give up their water in exchange for the goods and services negotiated. At the same time, the seller is happy to receive the water as payment for their goods and services.

Throughout history, humanity has used a number of commodities as money. However, virtually every commodity that was used had some type of issue, which made it unsustainable. Money needs to be divisible and fungible in order to actually serve as money. By "divisible," we mean that any currency which acts as money must be susceptible to division in equal parts without altering its natural composition. As for "fungible," this means that you don't necessarily need to receive the exact same unit of currency. Any other unit of currency that is of the same value will represent an equal amount of value.

To put these two points into perspective, consider the case of cattle as money. First of all, cattle are not divisible. This means that you cannot chop a cow in half to settle a payment. By the same token, not all cattle are the same. Some cattle are larger; others are fatter. This means that you cannot accept just any cattle as they do not represent the same kind of value.

Then, money is used as a store of wealth. This implies that when you hold on to it, money retains its value over time. In the case of cattle, a holder cannot keep it for a long time. In fact, cattle may simply grow old and die, thereby leaving the holder without their wealth.

Of all the commodities that humanity has used as money, the only two that have stood the test of time are gold and silver. These metals encompass all the characteristics that are needed for a commodity to function as money. That's why gold and silver have served as money for thousands of years.

However, there is a problem with physical gold and silver. In order for them to be used, they need to be mined out of the ground. This means that there is a limited supply of these metals available at any one time. Additionally, carrying a large amount of gold or silver, especially when settling a large account, can be inconvenient as it can be voluminous and heavy.

This is why countries figured out a way around it. The issuance of paper certificates to represent the value of gold and silver. Eventually, this system led to the creation of the famous "gold standard," that is, a country's currency is backed by a specific amount of gold and/or silver. In fact, this gold-backed currency system was in play until 1971. This means that up to about 40 years ago, all of the money in circulation around the world was fixed to a weight of gold.

Since then, gold and silver have been replaced by what is known as "fiat" currency. The term "fiat" refers to money issued by decree. As such, a government has the right to issue its own currency in order to for all transactions to be settled within the specific domain of that country.

This is why there is a market for foreign currency.

Since individuals do business with other individuals in other countries, there is a need to equate currencies based on their convertibility. These are the cross rates we have been referring to throughout this book.

Since fiat currency isn't backed by a physical commodity such as gold, there isn't any "real" backing behind it. Moreover, fiat currency's backing is based on the confidence that people have in it. So, as long as people believe it is valuable, it will be accepted as a means of settling accounts. When confidence falls, so does the value of the currency. This is when people stop accepting it as a means of payment and begin to demand a currency that does hold its value.

Furthermore, fiat currency is much more practical as it has led to the advancement of digital currency. As such, digital transactions can take place without the need for physical money. Although you can always go to an ATM and withdraw cash.

Still, the principles exploited in the use of digital fiat currency is what enables the creation of cryptos. Cryptos function in the same manner as regular currency insofar as it is backed by people's confidence. As long as people believe it to be an adequate store of value, they will be accepted as a means of settling accounts.

Lastly, cryptos solve one of the biggest issues that have haunted physical currency since the beginning of time. Since it does not physically exist, there is no real limit to the amount of currency that can be placed in circulation. Therefore, there could be an infinite money supply since there is no need to lug cash around. This facilitates the expansion of trade and financial services while also enabling citizens to keep their wealth store for extended periods. After all, a digital currency will never rust, break, or deteriorate over time. This makes it ideal for long-term storage.

The Decentralizing of Money

As noted earlier, the biggest advantage of cryptocurrencies is their decentralization. This means that cryptos are not subject to their issuances by a central bank or government authority. As such, cryptos are essentially created by the people and for the people.

However, this violates one of the main functions of central banks. In fact, it is a function that governments have fought very hard to impose upon their people. This is important to note as currency wasn't always issued by central banks or governments.

In fact, this is a relatively new concept.

In the past, most commercial banks could issue their own currency. In particular, banks that dominated a region could issue their own currency by way of banknotes. These banknotes could only be cashed in at the issuing bank.

The reason for these banknotes was based on the need to reduce the amount of physical gold and silver in circulation. So, bank customers could deposit their gold at a commercial bank and then issue banknotes as a means of paying other individuals. The individuals who received these notes could either cash them in for gold or use them to pay other individuals.

In a manner of speaking, it was like using a check that you received to pay someone else.

As commercial banks began issuing more and more notes, governments began cracking down on them as governments felt that commercial banks were infringing upon the sovereign right of the state to issue currency. That's why central banks came into being in the first place.

Do you see why governments aren't too crazy about cryptos?

On the whole, cryptos themselves do not infringe upon this government right. However, they are a direct competition for legal tender as folks would rather do business in a currency that is easy to use and not subject to taxation.

Herein lies the problem.

Governments aren't thrilled with the idea of cryptos gaining momentum, as this would imply accepting transactions that go beyond the traditional domain of taxing common transactions. This is why governments are yet to recognize any kind of validity of cryptocurrencies.

Furthermore, crypto breaks a central bank's monopoly over currency creation. This is what we mean by "decentralization." In fact, under the concept of the blockchain, virtually anyone can create their own currency in order to conduct any number of transactions. While this may provide unprecedented freedom, it can also cause havoc.

The reason why the proliferation of cryptos can lead to chaos is due to the lack of regulation. This means that clear rules need to be established in order for proper guidelines and procedures to be put in place. Without them, there would be no way that controversies could be solved, or rule could be enforced. Of course, the blockchain uses a set of rules which foster transparency, but the fact that there could be any number of cryptos in circulation makes it hard to keep score.

Additionally, having a large number of cryptos creates a situation in which it is hard to create a standard system of measurement. This is due to the fact that cryptos are measured differently, thereby making it hard to create a reasonable valuation for the goods and services in circulation.

Nevertheless, cryptos appear to be the largest step humankind has taken toward a fully digital monetary system that looks to decentralize government control over people's right to buy and sell the goods and services they need.

The Ban on Cryptos

The legality of cryptos is one of the hottest issues surrounding the cryptocurrency world. In essence, there are two sides to this discussion. Either you believe cryptos are legal or you don't. There really isn't any kind of middle ground in this discussion. For some folks, cryptos are perfectly legal and should not be banned. Others consider cryptos to be illegal as it is not an official government-issued currency.

However, determining the legality of cryptos boils down to a legal question that countries need to solve based on their current legal frameworks. This poses an interesting question as many countries do not outright ban cryptocurrencies. Yet, they don't explicitly authorize them either. This creates a legal vacuum that can be exploited by some unscrupulous folks.

In some countries, there is explicit legislation which either bans or authorizes the use of cryptocurrencies. In the countries in which cryptos are not explicitly outlawed, their use is limited to a certain set of transactions and situations. In other cases, their ban is total. This implies that anyone who is caught using cryptos for business purposes can be subject to prosecution.

While that may sound harsh, it makes perfect sense when you consider that governments will do everything they can to enforce their sovereignty over a country's monetary systems.

So, let's take a look at specific cases in which cryptocurrencies are considered legal.

In the European Union (EU), Bitcoin is considered to be a legal means of payment. However, it is not considered to be a currency. As such, it can be used to settle accounts and make payments despite the fact that it is not considered to be eligible for VAT when converting regular fiat currency to Bitcoin. However, transactions settle in Bitcoin are eligible for payment of VAT or sales taxes.

As for the G7 countries, guidance was issued in 2013 for companies dealing with digital currencies. While the G7 resolution did not explicitly grant permission for the use of digital-based currencies, companies were asked to follow applicable legislation in order to ensure proper adherence to financial regulations.

Interestingly enough, the United States declared Bitcoin to be legal in 2013 though it does not receive the status of a currency. Rather, it is considered to be a commodity and trades alongside other similar commodities like gold and silver. This implies that you can buy and sell Bitcoin through financial instruments as you would any other type of commodity.

In Canada, Bitcoin is legal and regulated by applicable legislation. However, there is a banking ban on the use of Bitcoin, meaning that customers are not permitted to conduct transactions using credit cards for the purchase of cryptos.

One clear case is that of Costa Rica. Costa Rica's laws do not recognize Bitcoin as a currency, as it is not backed by the government. By the same token, it is not illegal as it does not infringe any laws. Therefore, it's up to individual merchants to decide if they accept Bitcoin, or not.

In contrast, Bolivia and Ecuador have issued strict legislation banning Bitcoin outright. Other countries that have outlawed Bitcoin include Pakistan, Morocco, Egypt, and Algeria.

Ultimately, accepting Bitcoin (or any other crypto for that matter) as a means of payment appears to be a decision left up to individual merchants. This bodes well for the future of cryptos unless there is specific legislation down the road that reverses the current acceptance of cryptos.

State-Backed Cryptocurrencies

The idea of a state-backed cryptocurrency seems far-fetched at this point. In fact, most governments would rather not go near cryptos as they would much rather continue the issuance of fiat currency. However, the debate regarding governments getting into the crypto market has gained traction in the last few years.

One perspective on this matter is based on the premise of having governments issue their own cryptos so that private citizens are unable to do so. As such, the idea of government-issued cryptos seems to make a great deal of sense when you consider the practical use that could be given to such currencies.

In particular, the idea behind a state-backed crypto lies in moving away from physical currency into an entirely digital monetary system. When you think about it, we're a lot closer to that reality than you think. In fact, a great deal of financial transactions are just numbers of a computer screen. While you can still go down to the bank and get cash, the likelihood of that happening becomes less and less over time.

The fact is that it's much more practical to pay bills and make transactions by hitting a few keystrokes rather than carrying a wallet full of cash. Moreover, technologically-oriented folks would much rather use their phones and computers to do business rather than having to go through the complications of handling physical cash.

Still, the prospect of governments actually getting into the crypto market is still a long way away. One country that has expressed interest in an official crypto is China oddly enough. Given the fact that China is very much on the cutting edge of technology, it makes sense that they would be interested in issuing its own cryptocurrency. In fact, there has been talk of a gold-backed cryptocurrency. This crypto would be nothing more than digits on a computer screen. Nevertheless, the backing of this currency would be a fixed amount of gold. The purpose of this is to create confidence in the crypto itself, that is, give investors the impression that they are not being swindled by computer code.

Ultimately, it remains to be seen if this type of cryptocurrency would make sense. But there is no doubt that a cryptodollar or cryptoeuro is on the horizon. It's only a matter of time before governments wake up and realize there isn't much they can do to stop the emergence of cryptos. So, it's best to get with the program and take control before it's too late for governments.

The Future of Digital Currency

There is no question that digital currency is the way of the future. The question that is on the table is what digital currency will be like. The likeliest scenario at this point would be some kind of migration from traditional physical fiat currencies into a purely digital format.

As it stands, this would not be practical in much of the world. The majority of countries in the world still rely heavily on cash for the bulk of their transactions. And while the use of digital financial tools is rising, there is still a long way to go.

More and more, individual citizens are using digital means such as credit cards, e-banking, and third-party services like PayPal, Apple Pay, or Venmo, among many others. In fact, if you really tried to live a cashless life, you could certainly do it. Of course, some of your options would be limited. Still, there are plenty of ways in which you could go cashless.

When you think about it, the future of digital currency is wide open. In this case, though, we're not entirely clear what that future will look like. The emergence of the FinTech industry has provided investors with a clearer idea of what they can expect down the road. Still, there is a long way to go. The transition from physical currency to completely digital transactions requires the construction of a robust infrastructure that can handle the vast number of transactions that occur every day.

This means that a fully digital world would truly be something out of a science fiction movie. At the moment, it might seem unfathomable to think that not a single penny would exist, but then again, is that so hard to imagine?

It's important to keep in mind that the time to get into this market is now. Just like those savvy individuals who recognized an opportunity in Bitcoin way back in 2009, you have the opportunity to get in on the early days of this growing industry. You have the opportunity to really make your mark on the world by engaging the future of digital currency.

It's only a matter of time before governments realize that the blockchain, among other types of digital ledger technology, is the best way to ensure transparency among all people. It's a way of keeping folks accountable while establishing clear rules. So, it's best to get in on the action now, before it's too late. Once all the cards have been dealt with, it will be very hard for investors to make substantial gains. If experience has taught us anything, it's that having the vision to recognize emerging technologies before they become mainstream is the most effective way of capitalizing on a new trend. This is why we would encourage you to embrace cryptos before they take over the world market... for good!

CHAPTER 4

Trading Cryptocurrencies

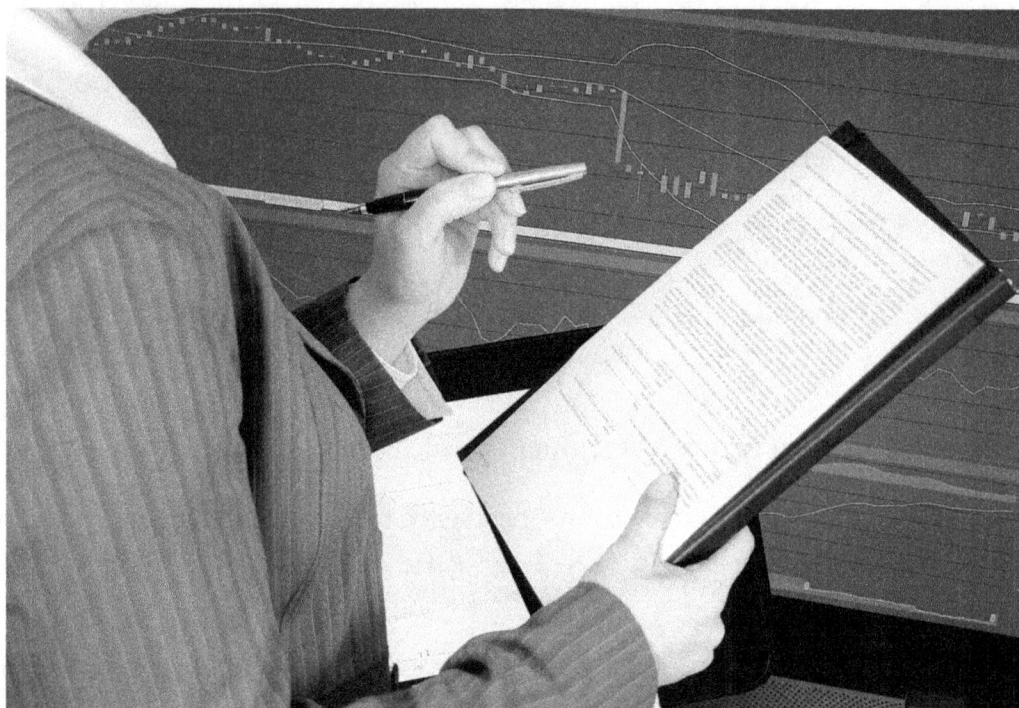

In this chapter, we are going to take a look at more specific aspects of cryptos and how you can get started with the fundamentals of trading cryptos. Additionally, we are going to discuss some very interesting issues which don't normally get addressed in regular investment literature.

In this regard, investing in cryptos can be a bit of a challenge. There are a number of factors that play into the valuation of cryptos while also making it tough to consider the importance of investor psyche. Consequently, you need to consider the importance that psychological factors have on the overall valuation of cryptos and how they can influence price and investment decisions.

In order to understand the valuation of cryptos, it's important to understand the dynamics of market forces and how they influence the price of any commodity and not just cryptos. As a result, we need to focus on a series of issues that underscore the importance of fundamentals in market conditions.

Also, we are going to specifically focus on Bitcoin, as this is the most commonly traded crypto. It's also the crypto that has gained the most notoriety around the world. Even though it has a rather limited supply, it's present all over the world. Consequently, investors from all walks of life are interested in seeing how they can make money off this little-understood commodity.

Why Is Bitcoin So Expensive?

This is a question for the ages.

In order to answer this question, it's important to look at Bitcoin as a commodity and not as a currency. This is a fundamental distinction as currencies and commodities trade quite differently.

In the case of currencies, these are subject to exchange rates. This means that you essentially convert one currency into another at a determined ratio. When you travel, you exchange your country's currency for that of the local currency of the country you are visiting. For most travelers, they first need to convert their country's currency into a major one such as US Dollars or Euros and then into the local currency of the county they are visiting.

When you speculate in currency exchange, you can make money from the increase or decrease in value of one currency in comparison to another. This is what the FOREX market is all about. Hence, the FOREX market has a completely different dynamic as the traditional stock market does.

With that in mind, looking at Bitcoin as a commodity means that it trades in the same way precious metals, agricultural goods, oil, and other goods that fall under this category. In addition, Bitcoin is also subject to the various investment vehicles that are available for commodities such as Exchange Traded Funds (ETFs), futures contracts, options, and straight buying and selling in the spot market.

Based on this premise, Bitcoin's valuation is rather straightforward. Simply put, there are investors who are willing to pay more than others for the right to hold Bitcoin. Moreover, the valuation of Bitcoin resembles that typical "bubble" that you often hear about on financial news channels.

In essence, a bubble consists of investors who want to get into an investment but without really understanding the underlying value of that investment. All they understand is that this investment is a great way to make money. As a result, they want to get in any way they can. That drives up the prices as holders of the asset are prepared to sell to the highest bidder.

This is exactly what happened to Bitcoin.

As investor realized the incredible potential of cryptocurrencies, they figured that getting into cryptos any way they could, would enable them to clean up when they eventually sold. This was true for the investors who got in early.

Way back in 2009, you couldn't give Bitcoin away. When it first began trading, it went for roughly $2 a coin. Yes, that's right, *two dollars*. It would take years for Bitcoin to get off the ground. When the blockchain and the potential for cryptocurrencies to become known, investors were willing to take a gamble on it. Those who had originally purchased at around $2 a coin, made a massive killing when coins began to sell at $200 apiece. From there, more and more investors had to get in.

Now, the reason why Bitcoin's price soared was its relative scarcity. Because of this, investors were willing to practically pay anything for a coin. But like all markets, it eventually leveled off. The ceiling for Bitcoin hit $20,000 a coin. At this point, the price simply become prohibitive for most investors.

Then, demand began to dry up.

Naturally, those who had already made a killing were reluctant to get back in. After all, why would they invest more money if they had already cashed out? This is where Bitcoin's price began to fall. From $20,000 a coin, it fell back down to about $2,000 a coin. At this price point, investors sought to get back in. Then, Bitcoin made a come up and jumped back up to $10,000 before falling back down.

Since the great boom and bust of Bitcoin, it generally trades between $5,000 to $8,000 a coin. On the whole, this fluctuation is due to the fact that investors seek safer assets when things get tough in the stock market. Alongside traditional safe-haven assets such as gold and bonds, investors are now looking at Bitcoin as a safe haven. Consequently, its price will go up and down based on investor demand.

How Is Trading Cryptocurrency Different From Regular Forex Trading?

Again, we must go back to the fact that Bitcoin trades like a commodity. As such, Bitcoin does not behave like a currency in the manner the Swiss Franc does. Bitcoin behaves in the same way that gold, coffee, and natural gas do. As long as there are investors who seek to purchase it, there will be a demand.

Let's take a look at an example of how a commodity is traded on the open market.

Oil is traded on the international market at a spot price. This means that the unit in which oil is traded (a barrel) has a specific price today. That price is used to negotiate the value of the contract. For instance, let's assume that a barrel of oil costs $50. This is today's price, and hence it is the spot price. When an investor wishes to purchase oil, they multiply the price by the number of barrels. That becomes the value of the contract.

However, oil cannot be delivered immediately; that is, it cannot be bought and then handed over right away. In the specific case of oil, a purchase made today is delivered roughly three months into the future. The same goes for agricultural products, metals, and practically any other commodity which doesn't already exist.

So, you are essentially purchasing a contract that's good for the delivery of the oil you have bought. This physical delivery will take place at the date specified in the terms of the contact. Please note that there are experts in the oil trade who have never even seen a barrel of oil in front of them. Yet, they trade in oil, make considerable amounts of money, and generate sound profits simply by trading contracts.

Additionally, the futures market is where commodities are bought and sold with a future date in mind. This means that you are locking in today's price (or whatever price you negotiate) on a deal that will take place at any point in the future. For instance, instead of the traditional 3-month time period, oil producers may negotiate contracts 6 months or even one year into the future. The reason for this is that these producers need cash to keep the lights on today. Investors trust these companies, and so they are willing to give them an advance on the overall value of the contract.

This is a general overview of how commodities are traded. This is an overview of how you can expect to trade Bitcoin on the open market. There is a spot market for Bitcoin, and then there is a futures market. When you put them together, there is a healthy "paper market" for them. We use the term "paper" as you are not dealing with the real thing; you are just selling the rights to it.

There is one other financial instrument that is used for trading commodities, which you need to be aware of: exchange traded funds (ETFs).

An ETF is basically an agreement under which a group of investors all pool their money and buy into a given commodity or group of commodities. These funds are managed by a firm, individual, or large financial institution to invest in a given product. The proceeds are then divided among the investor, while the investment firm keeps a percentage as a commission for their troubles. Some ETFs can be purchased through your regular broker, while others are "rich" clubs in which you need a certain net worth to get in.

Crypto ETFs have become popular in recent years. These investments give the general public exposure to cryptos without having to shell out $10,000 for a single coin. As such, small investors can get into the action even if they only invest a fraction of the cost for a single Bitcoin. Naturally, their share of the action is less. Still, it provides exposure to this market even when you may be just starting out with a few hundred dollars.

As a result, the main difference between crypto markets and FOREX is that cryptos are traded like commodities while FOREX trades like currency. With FOREX, you are swapping one currency for another at a determined exchange rate. This does not happen with cryptos. In addition, FOREX is a highly volatile market meaning that shifts in exchange rates can happen quite suddenly. And while regular commodities are subject to sharp movements in the market, the difference can be significant in the FOREX market is a very short timeframe.

So, you might be asking yourself, "are cryptos better than FOREX?"

The answer to that depends on what you are looking to gain. Frankly, FOREX requires much more active participation on the part of the investor. On the other hand, cryptos don't require a great deal of participation, especially if you take a passive approach, such as investing through an ETF. At the end of the day, it boils down on how much involvement you want in a specific investment. Hence, cryptos could be your best choice especially if you are simply looking to make money on the side.

The Best Cryptocurrencies to Trade

When looking to invest in cryptos, it's natural to be overwhelmed by the large number of coins out there. You might be enticed to take a flyer on coins value at a few dollars apiece. Who knows, they might turn out to be the next Bitcoin. But the likelihood of that happening is rather slim. Still, you could find some hidden gems if you look close enough.

But if you seek real value, then the following list will help you get ahead of the game.

1. **Bitcoin**. By far, this is the most popular crypto and the one with the most developed market. You can find all sorts of instruments ranging from the straight-up spot market to futures and ETFs. If you wish to gain exposure to it, but don't have the capital needed to make a significant investment, then an ETF might be the way to go.

2. **Ripple**. This is an affordable crypto that seems to be on the rise. In 2019, payment giant MoneyGram began using Ripple's blockchain to conduct transfers. This bodes well for Ripple as the coin itself may not be the most attractive aspect, but its proprietary technology is.

3. **Litecoin**. This crypto is generally mentioned in the same category as Bitcoin. While it doesn't have nearly as much exposure, you can certainly get in on the action. Individual Litecoins trade for less than a hundred dollars and are generally considered to have a great upside. It's already made a name for itself in the market. So, you can have reasonable assurance that you won't go wrong with this investment.

4. **Ethereum.** This is another of the big-league cryptos. The reason why Ethereum has such an incredible upside is due to the fact that its blockchain can be used for a multitude of projects. This makes its potential unlimited. While trading at less than $200 apiece, Ethereum is still affordable enough for newbies to get into the crypto space without breaking the bank.

5. **Neo.** Perhaps you haven't heard too much about Neo. It's relatively new on the scene, but it does hold some upside to it as it is an open-source technology. As such, it is a community-driven coin that seeks to optimize the flow of the digital economy. Be on the lookout for this one. Early investors saw their value double from around $7.50 a coin. Since then, it's settled to around $11.00 a coin. That's a pretty solid gain in the crypto world.

6. **Zcash**. Zcash's biggest advantage is its privacy protocols. It offers a higher degree of privacy than Bitcoin while enabling users to avoid tracking by government or private companies. It does have a fixed supply at the moment, 21 million coins, meaning that it does have the potential to spike in value. As of 2019, Zcash peaked at $112 per coin. Nevertheless, keep an eye out for this coin as it could follow the path of Bitcoin.

7. **Stellar**. This is a relative newcomer to the scene. It's been around since 2014 and aims to replace the aging SWIFT international banking network. It looks to create tokens that could facilitate international banking transactions in such a way that times could be reduced significantly.

8. **Cardano**. You may not have heard of this one. That's because it's only been around since 2015. However, it promises to deliver functionality for large-scale financial operations. Overall, it could lead to the possibility of a layered technology that would make updating seamless.

9. **Tron**. Tron is another newcomer. It's been around since 2017 and looks to provide a global network that would facilitate entertainment. This would enable free interaction among users. It has the potential to take over current world leaders like Netflix. Content creators would have a platform in which they could share and monetize their content freely and easily.

10. **Ontology**. This platform looks to integrate multiple chains. As such, it seeks to create simple solutions so that businesses can create ways of improving the reach of their business. So far, the Ontology network has a maximum output of 1 billion tokens.

Trends of Cryptocurrencies

To say that cryptos are on the rise is an understatement. Cryptos are clearly here to stay. The question then becomes: how to take advantage of cryptos?

To take advantage of the growing trend in cryptos, you need to play a dual role, both as a user and an investor. Firstly, if you already make use of digital banking services, then you are already well on your way to becoming a crypto user. The only difference between your current online banking and cryptos is the currency system itself.

This means that we can't really determine what using Bitcoin, Ethereum, or Litecoin will be like in terms of prices. It could be that buying a new car will cost you 10 Litecoins as opposed to $10,000. Nevertheless, these are minor changes when considering the functionality of cryptos.

It should be noted that the prices of cryptos do tend to fluctuate quite a bit. This is mainly due to the fact that these trade as commodities do. Thus, it's not easy to maintain stability in their pricing. Moreover, demand for cryptos at the moment is limited to a handful of investors. Even when the average user wishes to enter the crypto space, they may not necessarily have the means to do so. As a result, it can be somewhat complicated to get into the market at this point.

It is clear though, that the outlook for cryptos is a bright one. While we can't be sure about the amount of time it will take for cryptos to really catch on, the fact of the matter is that they are here to stay. So, it is now a matter of capitalizing on the upswing.

Getting Into Cryptocurrencies

If you are ready to take the plunge into crypto investing, then you should know that it isn't quite like picking up the phone and calling a broker. While you might find that some financial investment institutions do offer some kind of crypto investment fund, your best bet is to stay away from them.

To get into cryptos, there are two main ways. One is to purchase them directly from another user. This is like buying any kind of asset. All you do is pay the agreed price, and that's the end of it. However, these transactions are often fraudulent. So, you need to find a means of ensuring that the people you are dealing with are reputable. Otherwise, you may fall for a scam.

This is why the second way, and the best way, is to go through a coin exchange. These are online platforms in which you can buy and sell your coins easily and with the assurance that you are dealing with verified users. These exchanges include Coinbase, GDAx, and Bitfinex. These exchanges promote the fair exchange of coins while allowing users to make payments using credit cards and payment services like Apple Pay or PayPal. Of course, there are processing fees and commissions attached to these exchanges, so do keep them in mind.

The good thing about these exchanges is that they allow you to buy fractions of a coin. As such, you can buy a piece of a Bitcoin. This allows you to get into the action without having to shell out $10,000 for a single coin. If the price goes up, you make money. If the price goes down, then sit tight and wait for the rebound.

On the whole, getting into cryptos is quite easy. Plus, you don't have to deal with the number of regulations that come with regular investments in stocks and other financial instruments. Unless you have to know that you are dealing with a reputable individual, it's always best to go through and exchange. You have the assurance that you won't be swindled by an unscrupulous individual.

CHAPTER 5

Analysis Of Crypto Trades

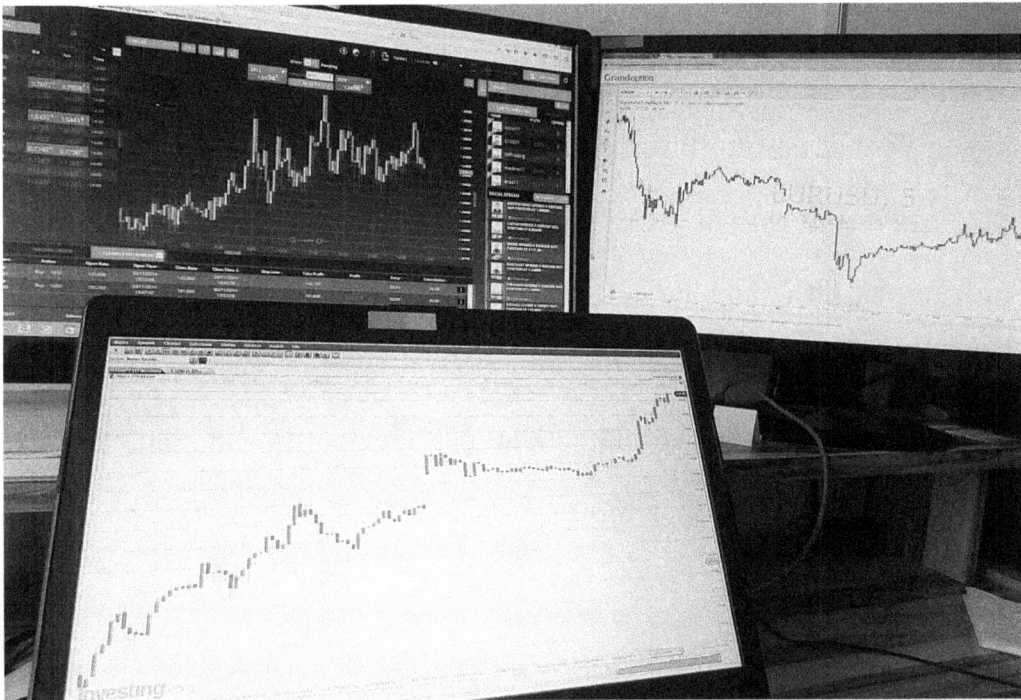

When looking to get started trading cryptos, it's important to become acquainted with the indicators that will help you track the progress and development of the price action related to cryptocurrencies. On the whole, these indicators are meant to be part of your technical analysis toolkit. They will provide you with the analytics you need to make rational decisions based on solid data. These data can help you complement your hunches. After all, it's important to have your instincts confirmed by the data. Otherwise, you may find yourself following a gut feeling that may, or may not, have any reasoning behind it.

If you are familiar with technical analysis in either stocks or FOREX, then you will find these analytics tools to be quite familiar. They are essentially the same though they are translated and honed for their use in the crypto market. Still, the fundamentals are quite similar. So, you should have no trouble adapting them accordingly.

In case you are brand new to the crypto market, fear not. The explanations provided in this chapter will enable you to get the most out of the information you will find in the charts and graphs described herein. Best of all, you will become quickly adept at identifying trends and patterns in the information seen in the charts and graphs in question. So, it's just a question of taking the time to review the fundamentals in order to get the most out of the information found in the technical analysis data pertaining to the crypto market.

Setting Up Indicators

The most important indicator that you need to become familiar with is **price**. That's the main indicator that will tell you how a particular crypto is doing. There is no question that price is your biggest friend. If you are able to make the right analysis of price action, you should be able to make sound decisions based on the amount of data available to you.

Let's consider this situation:

Price fluctuations are the result of the interaction between supply and demand. If you get into a crypto that is in high demand, the chances of you making good money are higher than if you get into a crypto that doesn't have a high demand. In such a case, you would need to be more patient. In contrast, cryptos that have a higher demand can be traded a lot more easily.

On the other hand, you might have a crypto that has a limited supply. In such cases, even when there isn't such high demand, the fact that there is a limited supply makes it more valuable. Such cryptos can offer you a good opportunity to make some money even when you may not be keen on holding onto your position for a long time.

When looking at price, please ensure that you have a look at the various timeframes that are available to you. Often, looking at a specific timeframe will only offer you a snapshot of what's actually going on in the market. In this case, you might be faced with a situation in which you are basing your assessments on incomplete data. So, it's always good to go back and review the data you have analyzed at various timeframes. This will enable you to get a better idea of the crypto's overall behavior patterns.

Another important indicator is known as the "moving average." This measure is calculated by tracking the average price of a crypto over a certain time period. This indicator can be calculated at any timeframe though the most common measurement is hourly. In the case of highly traded markets such as FOREX, it can be calculated on a minute-by-minute basis. However, this is not commonly done in crypto as cryptos don't have nearly as high trading volume. As a result, an hourly chart provides you with accurate information on the crypto's performance.

The moving average tracks the average between buy and sell prices. This is represented by candlesticks. These are the bars and move up and down the chart. Each candlestick represents the opening price at the bottom, the closing price at the top, and the length of the candlestick's body represents the margin between both prices. The longer the candlestick, the greater the difference.

Typically, the most common measure used for the purpose of tracking trend is the 10-day moving average. This average will tell you the average price of a crypto over a period of 10 days. This timeframe can then be further broken down into hourly segments. These hourly segments can help you pick up on any patterns that might be visible at certain times of day. It may seem incredible, but the time of day you trade has a significant impact on the results you stand to gain.

Other longer timeframes include the 20-day, 50-day, and 100-day moving average. All of these longer timeframes can be used to determine if there are any cyclical patterns in the price action of a crypto. For instance, there might be seasonal influence such as a downturn during summer vacation.

When looking into the technical analysis of cryptos, trading volume is an important indicator. By "trading volume," we are referring to the number of transactions that are completed during a specific time period. This indicator provides you with an idea of how commonly traded a crypto can be. In addition, trading volume is a good indicator that can determine the rise in demand for a specific crypto. When trading volume picks up, it can serve as a signal that more investors are becoming interested in any given crypto. As a result, you can make more trades, and thereby greater profits, based on the increased amount of movement in the crypto itself.

How to Analyze the Market

Analyzing the crypto market is done through the use of technical analysis tools. Unless you have access to a number of traders and investors, you won't be able to get a good feel for the market unless you look at the data.

Now, if you had access to investors and traders, you could simply talk to them and gauge the market. Even then, you would still be going on purely subjective data as one investor's sentiment may differ greatly from another. So, it's a question of ensuring that you have the numbers in plain view.

When it comes to analyzing the market, it's a question of understanding trends, ranges, and significant levels. These three items, in unison, will help you get a good idea of where the market is at the moment and where it may be headed down the road. As a result, you can't simply take one indicator; you need to look into all three indicators to help you get a good understanding of where the market will ultimately land.

In this regard, it's important to have access to as much technical data as you can. So, the first challenge becomes where to find the right data you need to conduct market analysis. There are many sources out there. So, it's best to have a discriminating eye when it comes to the information you are basing your decisions on.

Some of the major business news outlets such as Bloomberg, CNN, Money Watch, among others, may report on cryptos only as far as major news related to main cryptos such as Bitcoin and Ethereum. If anything, you may find information on crypto pricing specifically related to Bitcoin. Beyond that, getting detailed information can be a bit tough. This is why you need to consult website and market sources which are devoted especially to the crypto space.

Two sites that offer good information on the crypto space are CoinDesk and Coinbase. Both of these sites offer comprehensive information on pricing, volume, and supply. They can be a great place to start as far as getting updated information regarding the most relevant coins. Since there are thousands of coins in the market at the moment, it's virtually impossible to report on all of them. As such, you can get information on the most traded coins in addition to some lesser-known ones.

In the case of CoinDesk, this is an information service. As a result, you can expect to find a great deal of information regarding all things crypto. In this site, you can find just about everything you need to know with regard to the market. This is a great place to find current information. Also, it is a go-to reference site for crypto investors.

As for Coinbase, we mentioned earlier that this is an exchange. Therefore, you can buy and sell coins here. Consequently, Coinbase offers a great deal of information pertaining to the cryptos traded on their exchange. In this regard, the information may not be the broadest as it is essentially limited to the coins they offer. Nevertheless, there is a good deal of information. So, you can't go wrong with Coinbase.

Based on this, you can analyze the market in such a way that you can recognize the main indicators pertaining to the overall patterns of crypto prices. So, let's take a look at three indicators that you can deduce from the charts and graphs available to you on crypto pricing.

Trend in Price Action

In essence, trend is the direction in which the price is heading. Thus, using technical data on price action will allow you to determine this direction. On the whole, you can spot a trend just by looking at a chart. Price charts usually reflect price using a line graph. No other types of graphs are used as it is very difficult to graphically represent price using any other means.

When you look at a price chart, you'll see quite a bit of points. Some go up, and some go down. Generally speaking, this does not represent trend itself as the price action may indicate a great deal of fluctuation. Nevertheless, you can determine trend by taking a closer look at the information contained in the chart.

You can do this by looking at the direction in which the curve is moving. In some cases, the curve appears to be moving upward. This is known as a "bullish" trend. Then, you may spot the curve moving in a downward direction. This is known as a "bearish" trend.

A bullish trend means that the price is moving upward. As a result, the crypto in question is gaining in value in relation to Dollars, or perhaps another currency. On the other hand, a bearish trend means that the crypto is losing value in relation to another currency or crypto.

Determining the actual trend of the data can be done in two ways. The first is the trendline that is generated by the chart itself. Most price charts do this automatically. Otherwise, you would have to take the data in table form, input it into a spreadsheet program like Microsoft Excel, and then calculate your own trendline. While doing these calculations yourself is more time-consuming, you can be certain about the numbers you see when you do the math yourself.

Another way in which you can determine the trend in a data set is by joining the lowest point of a curve with its highest point with a straight line. The line will reveal an upward or downward slope. This is the trend. Then, you can see the various points in which the line intersects with the markings on the chart. These are all potential price points that you can use to determine your buy or sell points. It's important to note that this approach is not 100% accurate as you are simply making a manual trace. However, it is very useful when determining trend in a data set. Plus, it's great when you are simply looking at data and don't have a lot of time to actually sit down to crunch the numbers.

Of course, it's best to have an automatically generated trendline by the chart itself. Nevertheless, the methods that we have outlined here will help you to spot trend easily and effectively.

Ranges or Bands in Price

When you hear the term "range" or "band," you need to think about price action within a specific upper and lower limit. This means that prices do not exceed these limits. For instance, XYT crypto is trading "in a band." This means that the lower limit of the band is $1 while the upper limit is $5. This implies that you can expect to see its price range anywhere from $1 to $5. However, you cannot expect to see the price fall below $1 or exceed $5. If that were to happen, then you could be experiencing an unusual opportunity.

There are times when a crypto trades in a "narrow band." This means that the price does not move very much either way. For example, the price can range from $1 to $1.05. The range here is 5 cents on the Dollar. Depending on the usual price action, the band could be even narrower. Sometimes, the band is so narrow that changes are measured in amounts less than a penny.

Now, you might be thinking, "how can you make money if a crypto is making less than a penny?"

The answer to that is numbers.

You see, when you trade in large amounts, say hundreds or even thousands of coins, then you can make some significant gains. Let's assume that the gain on a coin has been a penny. Yet, you sell 10,000 of them. That's a $100 profit. That may not seem overwhelming, but it is certainly profitable when you are able to make the same trade over and over again. When you multiply $100 over say, 10 or 12 transactions, now you have about a $1,000 in your pocket.

To identify that a crypto is trading in a band, you can look for one of two types of trendlines.

The first is a horizontal trendline that is moving sideways. This means that it has very little to no upward or downward slope. If it is completely flat, then you have a crypto that might be moving in an extremely narrow margin. To take advantage of this trend, you would need to go back in time to see where the price of this crypto was sitting. It could be that it dropped, it is now trading sideways and perhaps gaining momentum before taking off. On the other hand, it could be that it climbed, leveled off and may drop back down. The important thing to notice is the direction it was headed prior to leveling off. This can give you some indication of what's to come.

The second type of trendline is a curve that fluctuates up and down in the same range. This means that there is some predictability in the levels the curve will hit. When this occurs, you can be relatively sure of how far up the price will rise, and then how far down the price will fall. Under this type of model, you can safely plot your entry and exit points.

You can take advantage of this band by entering at the lowest point and selling at the highest. You may not be profiting a great deal on individual trades, but you might be able to really make some good money by exploiting that band multiple times over.

Significant Levels: Resistance and Support

One of the most important aspects of recognizing trading patterns is understanding significant levels. When we discuss these levels, we are focusing specifically on support and resistance levels. These are vitally important when considering the importance they bear on the overall way of determining price action.

Let's start by discussing what a "support level" is. In essence, a support level is the bottom or "floor" in the price of a crypto. This means that the price action will drop to this price level but not go any lower. This is important to note as support levels generally serve as a psychological barrier in which investors feel comfortable entering the market. This level serves as the base from which price action then reverses trend (usually downward) and then begins to climb back up to the high point.

It should be noted that support levels are not ironclad. This means that it is quite possible that the price will break through the floor. When this occurs, a new support level may be set. As such, you need to be keen on the price action. If you are holding on to a crypto during a breakthrough, you may end up having to hold on to the coins longer than anticipated as you wait for the price to recoup.

The high point of a price action data set is known as a "resistance level." By "resistance," we mean that investors are reluctant to pay more than a certain price for a crypto. At this point, most investors being to liquidate their position. As such, the trend reverses and begins a downward slope all the way back down to the support level. Like support, resistance is a psychological barrier in which investors feel satisfied selling their coins. However, if demand is high, investors may decide to hold on longer in hopes of getting a higher price.

When price surpasses a resistance level, you have what is known as a "breakout." A breakout is an investor's dream come true. When the price of a coin breaks out, there is no telling how high it can go. As such, you may find that if price surpasses your expectations by a wide margin. However, it should be noted that breakouts are rather uncommon. So, it's important to spot the signs so that you can ride that wave.

On the whole, this interaction between support and resistance levels can be clearly observed when a coin is trading in a band. The price rises to its resistance level and bounces back down all the way to the floor and then rebounds back up to its ceiling (resistance level). This can happen multiple times over the course of a trading day or even multiple days. This level of predictability can make it very easy to make consistent profits. So, it's definitely worth keeping in mind.

CHAPTER 6

Developing Trading Algorithms

When you read about developing trading algorithms, you will generally run into a very technical discussion on coding and software programming. Yes, trading algorithms do involve coding. This means that if you wanted to fully automate your trading, you would have to have the requisite IT skills needed to program the computer to do what you want it to do.

In fact, large institutional investors invest the money needed to produce these algorithms. The reason for this is that these large investment firms would rather pay a programmer once to develop a program rather than pay a broker over and over to trade for them.

Additionally, trading algorithms allow investors to automate their strategies. This means that there is no need for a human to be constantly entering information. The machine takes care of the process. However, there is still a need for human oversight, especially if things aren't going well.

As for retailer investors, that is, investors who have smaller investment capital, using algorithmic trading doesn't mean you need a degree in computer science or pay a ton of cash to a software developer. You can develop your own algorithms based on your knowledge and experience. As a result, you can make the most of your talents and abilities along with reliable data. This is why we are going to explore how you can make your trading algorithm so that you can facilitate trading. It should be noted that the principles described here apply, not just to cryptos, but to all financial assets. This means that these concepts can be extrapolated to stocks, FOREX, and commodities, among others.

Developing or Fine-Tuning a Strategy

The first thing you need in order to get started with algorithmic trading is to develop a strategy. This means that you need to know what you want to do even before you begin devising the nuts and bolts of your algorithm.

There are two main approaches that you can follow when it comes to devising your own trading algorithm.

The first is known as "high-frequency trading" or HFT. In HFT, what you are essentially doing is making the same trade over and over. What this allows you to do is make a profit on multiple transactions within a short timeframe. This leads you to multiply profits in quick succession so that they add up over time.

On the whole, HFT implies that you make small returns on each transaction. However, the high number of transactions conducted adds up, leading you to accumulate a significant return. This type of trading is very good for assets that are trading in a band. As such, if you find that your coin of choice is trading in a rather predictable band, you can exploit this trading to make sense for you. In the end, you rack up small profits, but multiply them over the total number of transactions conducted.

The other approach you can apply in this case is value investing. Value investing consists of finding undervalued coins which have the potential to rebound. In this case, you observe a coin that is trading below its usual market value. Then, you sell when the time is right.

This type of trading approach requires a good deal of research as you need to understand both the usual value of a coin in addition to its dynamic. For example, you have a coin that generally trades for $1. However, you find that its valuation suddenly falls to about $0.95. Upon seeing this, you realize that you are getting a good deal at this point. So, you decide to scoop it up in hopes that its valuation will return to its average of $1. Since the coin is undervalued (there are many reasons why this can happen), all you need to do is sell at $1 or slightly above it to make a profit.

This approach requires careful planning and attention to detail, even though the transaction itself is rather straightforward. The main thing here is to keep a close eye on the value of the various coins you are tracking. Once you find an undervalued coin, you pounce on it. When the price goes back up, you can sell for a profit.

It is really that simple. The hard part is finding the right coins at the right price. Therefore, this approach does not allow you to make a large number of transactions. In fact, the number of transactions you would be making is far less than in HFT.

Also, value investing is more of a manual process. However, you can use algorithmic trading to help you spot the values that you want in order to help you automate the process. As such, you won't have to pour over charts all day long to find what you seek. All you need to do is set up the right price points.

Now, the good news about algorithmic trading is that trading platforms allow you to enter the parameters of the deal you want to make happen. This is great because you can simply enter the entry and exit points, and you are good to go.

In the specific case of FOREX, trading platforms are well-equipped to serve this type of purpose. You can fully automate your trading system by entering the parameters that you want. If the price action hits these parameters, the deal is executed. If not, the deal does not happen. This can certainly help you stay on top of a situation, especially when you are not planning to be physically at your computer.

The caveat to algorithmic trading is that you cannot simply set it up and forget about it. You need to check in on it every once in a while. Usually, this might mean every hour or so. When you fail to check your automatic trading setups, the algorithm can run amok. This is especially true when trading volume picks up. If this is the case, then you might end up triggering the opposite effect of what you wish to achieve.

For instance, you have set up a very low entry point as you expect to pounce on a valuable coin. And while the entry point is triggered, the exit point is not. This means that your sell price is never hit. Thus, the sale of the coin never happens. Thus, you end up holding on to the coin much longer than anticipated. To make matters worse, the price keeps dropping. Since you weren't paying attention, the value keeps dropping and dropping, thus costing you a larger amount of money.

Do you see why you need to keep tabs on your automated positions?

Of course, this might be a bit of an extreme scenario. Nevertheless, it does happen. So, it's best to always keep tabs on any open positions you may have.

Making Use of Trendlines

As we have discussed throughout this book, trend is an integral part of your trading strategy. So, it only makes sense to automate this part of the process. Earlier, we talked about how you can manually calculate trendlines to ensure that the data you are analyzing is right. While this is certainly valid, the fact of the matter is that most investors don't have the time to sit down and pour over charts and tables. Sure, there is a great sense of satisfaction that comes with running the numbers yourself. But when it comes to trading cryptos, time really is money.

The easiest way to calculate trendlines is to simply enable this function in the charts you generate. This is, by far, the easier way. Best of all, this is done automatically for you. So, you don't have to actually worry about generating trendlines.

Once you have generated trendlines, you can use them to determine entry and exit points as part of your strategy. For instance, you can set up an entry point at the exact point where a bearish trendline touches the support level. By the same token, you can set up an exit point right when a bullish trendline touches on a resistance level.

You can easily spot these in the charts you generate. Then, all you need to do is enter these points in your trade configuration. This will alert the platform to execute these deals when these points are triggered.

That's all.

Of course, keep tabs to make sure the price action is trending in the direction you have identified. If something should go wrong, don't hesitate to pull the plug. Please bear in mind that it's always best to cut your losses as soon as possible.

Acceleration of Trend

One important aspect about trend is the pace on which it is moving. By "pace," we're referring to the time it will take for a given price point to be hit. A good rule of thumb to keep in mind here is that the sharper the slope, the faster the time. This means that a trendline that is essentially horizontal will take far longer to hit certain points compared to one that's practically vertical. Of course, perfectly horizontal and vertical trendlines are impossible. What is true is that there are sharply inclined lines which you can use to tell you the pace of trend.

When you are looking at trendlines, it is possible to spot an acceleration or deceleration of trend. While the trendline doesn't actually reflect these shifts directly, you can confirm this increase or decrease in pace by the way the overall price action looks.

When looking at price action, in this case, you'll find the curve that is traced as part of the price action chart suddenly jumps up or falls down. In this case, you can quickly spot the potential acceleration or deceleration point. When you compare that to the trendline, you'll be able to determine if there is a change in pace.

Another indicator that you can use to confirm your visual appreciation is trading volume. You can quickly spot trading volume through a combination of another line graph or a histogram. A histogram is a bar chart that plots the number of transactions completed over certain intervals. For instance, the histogram chart can plot these changes on an hourly basis. These spikes in trading volume should coincide with the spikes in price action.

One very interesting aspect of trading volume is that you will find it to be repetitive. This means that there are certain times of day or certain days in the month where action tends to pick up. These increments in trading volume are generally associated with specific events like the weekend, payday, after working hours, and so on.

Graphical Analysis

Crypto investors who do not take advantage of graphical analytics tools are doomed to suffer from bad trades. The reason for using graphical analysis tools lies in the fact that you cannot accurately detect price movements without some sort of analytical tool that can help you spot patterns.

Now, it should be noted that you don't have to live and die by charts alone. There are other factors that are involved in determining the valuation. For instance, there are psychological factors that affect investors' decisions. Nevertheless, these elements are always reflected in price. If an event is noteworthy, it will eventually be reflected in price action.

What does this mean?

It means that using charts to your advantage is essential in getting a head start on the market. The best graphical analysis tools allow you to run simulations on future behavior based on current information. These tools, while hardly perfect, give you a pretty accurate picture of what you can expect down the road, given the patterns seen at the moment.

These tools are great, especially when you are dealing with a crypto that's trading in a band. This high level of predictability makes it quite easy for you to make a profit even if it's not mind-blowing. Furthermore, you can plan ahead without having to second-guess yourself.

Additionally, graphical analysis allows you to conduct "backtesting." Backtesting refers to testing your models and assumptions on prior data. This is great because it allows you to see if your trade setups would have worked previously. As such, you can see if the price action for that specific coin will reinforce your assumptions. If you are proven wrong, then you can tweak your setup to reflect the real data.

It should be noted that backtesting and forecasting work when there isn't a high degree of volatility. Volatility means that there are significant swings in price action in a short timeframe. Generally speaking, high volatility is the result of increased trading activity, especially when investors are rushing to enter the market or looking to dump their positions. As such, you'll see wild upswings or downturns in price action.

If you are seriously looking to become a successful investor, then making the most of graphical analysis tools will enable you to make some serious gains without having to bet the farm on a hunch.

Reversal Pattern

All successful investors become adept at spotting when trend is about to reverse. This means spotting when a downward trend will switch to an upward one and vice-versa. Learning to spot trend reversal is quite useful when it comes to maximizing profit.

The underlying principle here is to buy at the lowest point and sell at the highest.

This works very well when you are in a predictable pattern, such as when a coin is trading in a range or band. So, the challenge then becomes identifying when the reversal will actually take place.

Let's consider this situation.

You are tracking the price of coin BTF. This coin is currently trading at a support level of $1.05 and a resistance level of $1.15. This means that there is a 10-cent spread among levels. Theoretically, you could get in at $1.06 and still make money. However, this is not the optimal entry point, as you could have gotten in lower. Consequently, you could have maximized your gain had you gotten in at a lower point.

By the same token, you could exit the trade at $1.09 and still make money. Again, this is not the optimal exit point, as you could have made more profit by leaving at a higher point. This is why the challenge is to spot the lowest entry point and the highest exit point. This is how you can maximize your profit.

Of course, it is virtually impossible to get in at the lower mathematical point. Also, it's quite difficult to exit at the precise moment the highest price point is hit. Unless you are dealing with a coin that is trading in a very predictable band for a long time period, this can be quite tough to determine. Nevertheless, you can still get in at a very favorable point while leaving at a highly profitable one.

So, let's look at how you can accurately spot these reversal points given a data set on a price action chart.

First, take any coin you wish to study. Generate a price action chart that is about 24 hours old. It's best not to use current information as this may change rapidly. So, using charts that are 24 to 48 hours old can be a good place to start.

Then, generate the trendline. Make sure it overlaps on the actual price action curve. This will allow you to intersect the various points in the chart with the trendline itself. Also, ensure that the trendline shows a clear bullish or bearish trend. If you have a sideways trendline, you might be better off going back further in time or just looking at another coin.

Next, take a good look at the points in which the trendline intersects with the support and resistance level. The rule of thumb is the following:

When you have a bearish trendline, that is a downward trendline, the point in which this line touches the support level will indicate the point at which a reversal to a bullish trend will take place. Likewise, a bullish trendline that intersects with the exact point of a resistance level would signal the reversal in trend to a bearish one.

This is how you can determine the entry and exit points of a trade, particularly when you are dealing with a coin that's trading in a band. As such, you can make some easy profits in such situations.

Lastly, backtest your strategy several times over using different timeframes. If you find that there is a predictable pattern repeating over and over, you could have a good option that you can trade on a regular basis. However, if you spot that your pattern doesn't hold up very well over time, then you would need to pay close attention to the signals that would indicate the reversals you need in order to enter and exit a trade.

Head and Shoulders Pattern

The head and shoulders pattern is a standard of technical analysis. This pattern is generally used to identify a potential reversal in a bearish or bullish trend. As such, it can be used to track changes in the overall trend of a given data set.

This pattern is characterized by a price action curve that has three distinct spikes. These spikes are what serve to create the head and shoulders pattern. As such, you have one peak (the first shoulder), then a larger spike (the head), followed by a third, smaller peak (the second shoulder). When this pattern emerges, you'll quickly see the reverse in trend.

Let's consider the following example:

The overall price action has been on the positive side. This has been evidenced by the price action hitting the resistance level multiple times. Then, there is a sharp spike that broke out of the resistance level before returning back down to its average. The next spike hit the resistance level and moved back down.

While this may appear to be bullish, the trendline indicates there is a downward trend. As a result, you can expect there to be a reversal in the overall trend. The reversal will be evident by a breakthrough in the support level. This means that the price will fall through the floor once the price action curve hits bottom. From there, it is uncertain how far the price will fall.

Generally speaking, following a breakthrough, the new floor is seen after the price bounces back up and then hits the same point on the floor. If you see two or three consecutive hits around the same point on the floor, then you can be relatively certain a new floor has been established. It could be that there is a new band in place, or you may expect another reversal.

In this example, the exact point in a reversal is evidenced by a succession of long candlesticks right before hitting the floor. Then, there will be one very short candlestick following the long ones. When you see this short candlestick, the reversal is about to take place.

This is the point where you can anticipate the reversal coming. If you are looking to enter a trade, this is not the best time to do it. You may end up seeing a huge drop in price before seeing a significant rebound. As such, you may have to hold on for a while before recouping your position.

The opposite case is the exact inversion. This is where you have troughs instead of peaks highlighted by a bullish trendline. This means that the price action has been low, but looks to rebound and look for a breakout.

In this case, you have a short trough punching down on the floor, then a breakthrough, followed by another punch on the floor. Just like the previous case, the reversal will come when you see a succession of long candlesticks followed by a very short one. At that point, the reversal will mean a breakout past the previous high. Now, how high the breakout will go is uncertain. You can look at previous history to get an idea of where the price may land.

It should be noted that head and shoulders with a bearish trendline needs to have clearly defined resistance levels. However, it is not required to have a clearly defined support level. By the same token, the head and shoulders pattern with a bullish trendline needs to have a clearly defined floor but not necessarily a clearly defined ceiling.

Ultimately, it's up to you to decide how low or how high you think the price action will go. When you anticipate a breakthrough, you can get in at the very low end of the trough. If you anticipate a breakout, you can sell at the highest possible point you have determined. However, a good rule of thumb is to play it conservatively. That way, you won't hold on for too long, thereby risking your profit margin.

Triple Top and Triple Bottom

The pattern known as "triple top" or "triple bottom" can serve one of two purposes.

The first is to confirm a support or resistance level. When there is a high degree of volatility or a reversal in trend, you need to find some sort of indication that there is a new support or resistance level emerging. Until you can get this confirmation, you can't be entirely sure about where the price action will ultimately land.

This is where you can use this pattern to establish if there is, in fact, a support or resistance level.

Let's consider triple tops. Following a reversal in trend from bearish to bullish, you want to establish if there is a new resistance level in place. So, you observe the peaks to find that three consecutive hits have been identified at, or close to, the same point. This can be taken as an indication of a resistance level. However, official confirmation cannot be made until you look at the candlesticks. When you look at the candlesticks, you can see a series of at least three candlesticks of roughly the same size. Then, as the price action curve begins to descend, you have a good idea of what the new resistance level looks like. As long as the trendline remains bullish or begins to level off, you can be sure that you are in a new range with a clearly defined resistance level.

In the opposite case, there are three successive bottoms following a trend reversal. As long as the same conditions apply, you can infer there is a new support level in place. This can help you determine solid entry points.

The second purpose is to spot a breakout or breakthrough. When you see three successive tops with a sharp trendline, you might be gearing up for a breakout. To get more confirmation on this, look at the trading volume. If the volume has been lower than usual, then you can expect pressure to build. Once the trading volume takes off, you can expect the breakout to take place.

The same goes for triple bottoms. When the trading volume seems to be on pause, the three successive bottoms may give you an indication that investors are only waiting for a signal to begin selling. As such, you need to pay close attention to when the trading volume picks up again. When this occurs, the price may breakthrough giving you an opportunity to pick up some good bargains.

On the whole, this pattern is rather easy to spot. The three consecutive peaks or troughs ought to provide you with enough forewarning of the break in the previous significant level. By paying attention to the triple top or bottom, trendline, and trading volume, you have all of the technical analysis indicators you need to really make sense of the price action you are seeing.

As you become more and more experienced in trading, you will be able to recognize these patterns more easily. As a result, you'll be able to make significant gains even when others may be afraid to enter the market.

CHAPTER 7

Risk Management

Risk is an inherent part of investing. Any time you choose to invest in anything, stocks, bonds, FOREX, commodities, and crypto, there is risk that is associated with it. You cannot escape it. It's there, and you need to address it accordingly. If you believe that risk is something you can skirt around, you'll be disappointed to find it biting you at some point down the road.

On the whole, risk is a question of things not working out the way you had planned. This means that you need to deal with the fact that things may not go your way at any given point in time. As such, managing risk becomes a question of figuring out what to do with it. Since you can't escape it, then the only thing you are left with is trying to understand how you can minimize its potential impact on your investment portfolio.

This is why the term "risk management" boils down to taking preventive measures that you can use to reduce the likelihood of being negatively impacted by unforeseen occurrences. These occurrences can range from mistakes in your trade setup to the so-called "black swans" that is, totally unexpected events that can cause a severe impact on your trading.

In this chapter, we are going to take a look at risk management and how it pertains to cryptocurrencies. On the whole, you'll see how risk management is a question of minimizing risk by making sound investment decisions. Therefore, we're not talking about a magic shield that will keep you safe and sound. We're talking about sound investment practices which will keep negative consequently at bay.

The Role of Brokers

Brokers are licensed professionals who are trained in money management. These individuals are trained to make investment decisions on behalf of their clients. As such, they are legally bound to make the best decisions they can be based on the information that they have available. However, please keep in mind that brokers are really only looking out for themselves. What they are really after is building their bonus. This means that they don't actually care about *you* making money; they only care about making money for themselves.

Now, in terms of risk management, you can hire a professional broker to manage your investments. In doing so, you are reducing your risk as you are handing over your investment decisions to someone who is fully invested in the trading world. In the end, all you get is a statement and a check for your earnings. But, is this truly the best you can do?

Sure, you cut risk down by trusting someone who is trained and experienced in the world of investing. But that comes at a price. In addition to the commission that you must pay to your broker, you are also on the hook for taxes and account fees. In the end, your potential earnings are whittled down by the large amount of commissions and fees you need to pay.

Needless to say, this is not the wisest investment decision you can make. As such, you are handing your money over to someone else so that they can use it to pad their own pockets. Meanwhile, you'll be lucky if you get a check large enough to fill your car's tank.

Now, if after reading this book so far you feel that simply hiring an investment professional would make life easier for you despite all the fees, then so be it. Perhaps you feel you may not have enough time to dedicate to the rigors of trading crypto. Perhaps you feel that it's just easier to pay the fees as that would save you a ton of work.

If you have an investment capital large enough, it will probably make sense. We're talking about hundreds of thousands of dollars, if not millions. However, if you are a retail investor looking to build your own path, then handing over your hard-earned cash to a broker doesn't make sense.

In addition, if you choose to invest in an ETF or a mutual fund, then you are better off simply putting your money under the mattress. These vehicles, while generally safe, deliver highly underwhelming returns. In particular, mutual funds are indexed to the stock market. As a result, they are dependent on the overall conditions of the market. If the market is down, you'll take a pounding. If the market is rocking and rolling, then you'll make money.

That doesn't sound like the best investment strategy you could make.

So, if you are ready to cut out the middleman and make some real money, then read on.

No Brokers for Crypto

There are no brokers, no funds, no middlemen when it comes to crypto. It's you and your money. This means that you have the means to make your own destiny in this market. Sure, there have been some so-called crypto ETFs popping up in various investment companies. However, they offer very underwhelming returns. These are not the type of returns you seek to make.

When you engage in the world of crypto trading, you will find that the money you make is yours. In some instances, you won't even be liable for taxes. Although, it's always best to check in your state to make sure that you have the right information as you may be on the hook for some tax payments.

Since there are no middlemen, you stand to make some good money as there are no fees and commissions to be paid. Now, it should be noted that the exchange on which you trade your coins may charge you a fee per trade. This fee is tied to the number of trades you make. So, if you make zero trades, you don't have to pay anything. However, if you make a billion trades, then you would have to fork over the corresponding sum.

In the greater scheme of things, paying a fee per trade is much better than paying a fee, commission, and account management dues. That just doesn't make sense. Plus, why would you have your money invested in stocks, especially when the market isn't in the best possible shape? When you really think about it, investing in cryptos makes a lot more sense, especially when you are looking to avoid much of the drama that comes with traditional investing.

Now, there is one catch to the crypto market. Since it doesn't have nearly as much regulation as the traditional stock market or FOREX, you need to be sure you are dealing with trustworthy sources. This means that if there is any kind of dispute regarding transactions, you are pretty much on your own. That is why you need to make sure that you know who you are dealing with.

Beyond that, the crypto space can be a wide-open field for you to make some serious returns. In addition, cryptos give you the opportunity to take control of your investment decisions. This is a powerful aspect for the average investor. By taking control of your investment portfolio, you can make the best possible decisions based on your objectives and expectations.

Cryptocurrency Wallet

Cryptos are stored in a digital wallet or vault. This is important to note. These are just files which you can store on your computer. Of course, you could if you wanted to. However, there is always the case of risk to consider. Therefore, using a digital wallet that is offered by a reputable provider makes the most sense.

As mentioned earlier, cryptos are nothing more than a sequence of computer code. That sequence is used to conduct the transactions for which it was designed. As a result, it is not the wisest idea to simply store it as a regular file on your computer. This implies that you need to find a good way of storing it securely.

Crypto exchanges like Coinbase offer a digital vault service. They don't charge you anything for storing your coins. After all, they gain by keeping the stash in the house. In a manner of speaking, it's like a regular bank that doesn't necessarily need to have cash on hand to cover all of their customers' deposits. After all, the likelihood of all customers wanting their money at the same time is rather slim.

The same goes for crypto vaults.

So, a vault service such as the one provided by Coinbase can be a good alternative for savvy investors. This reduces the amount of exposure your coins have to would-be thieves. Plus, all you need is a password to access your wallet.

Speaking of passwords, it's important for you to make sure that you make provisions for your password to be transferred to your heirs in case of your passing. If you happen to pass on unexpectedly, your heirs may never be able to access your coins. In fact, the exchange wouldn't even be able to access them as they don't have the authorization to access your coins. Hence, it's a good idea to make these kinds of provisions well in advanced.

Wallet Security

The biggest recommendation that is generally made regarding wallet security is safeguarding your password. Passwords used to access digital wallets tend to be highly complex in order to prevent thieves from getting their greedy paws on your coins. As such, it's always best to make sure your password isn't easy to crack.

When you go about opening an account for your digital tokens, finding a reputable company is always the best choice. Even if you need to pay an extra bit of cash to keep your coins safe, in the end, it's totally worth it. You can't expect to safeguard your coins by having the cheapest service in the market. In fact, when it comes to digital wallets, you get what you pay for. This means that finding the right balance between cost and security is fundamental.

The consensus best overall wallet is Coinbase. We have mentioned this company several times throughout this book since it is considered to be the best in the industry. Since Coinbase also functions as an exchange, you can purchase your coins and store them directly. Plus, you don't have to pay a dime for the wallet itself. This is an added bonus. Other wallet companies include Trezor, Ledger, SoFi, Robinhood, Edge, and Exodus. These are all reputable companies though it's important to make sure that you do your homework on hacks and attacks that might have been made to any of these companies. Please keep in mind that thieves are always looking for vulnerabilities. So, it's always a good idea to do an online search to see just how reliable they have been. For instance, Robinhood was famously hacked some time ago. Although the company denied any customers' wallets being affected, it just goes to show that any company can be the subject of an attack at any time. This is why we strongly recommend that you double-check with companies before engaging with them.

Wallet Hacks

In theory, you could build your own digital wallet and use your computer as a storage device. However, any time your computer goes online, you are technically vulnerable to an attack. Therefore, your computer, as such, is not the best place to store any of your tokens.

One solution that some investors have found is to store their coins on an external hard drive. Since this hard drive is offline, would-be thieves have no access to it. Therefore, you can be safe that no one is going to try and steal your coins.

However, there is one catch. If you choose to store your coins in this manner, you wouldn't be able to access them readily. Thus, you need to make sure that you can access your coins rather easily, especially if you are looking to buy and sell on a regular basis. Now, if you are planning on purchasing them and simply holding on to them, then storing them in an offline device would make sense.

With that in mind, the biggest attack of your digital wallet would be through the use of malware intended to steal your password. You can download this type of malware from any number of places. Hence, having a good firewall program also comes in handy.

On the whole, your digital wallet can be hacked if you are not careful with your password. Beyond that, the only other way that your wallet could be hacked is if the vault company is hacked. While this is entirely possible (as the Robinhood case), these companies need to ensure their customers' safety.

To put the biggest heists into perspective, here is a choice list of the biggest digital wallet hacks know to date. First, Bithumb was taken for $30M worth of coins. Also, Coinrail was hit for $37.2, BitGrail $195M, and Coincheck was knocked around for $534M. This is nothing to sneeze at, to say the least. These hacks have been perpetrated by notorious international hackers. And while the companies vowed to restore their customers' coins, the loss in market value is indeed massive.

Exchange Hacks

Just like wallet hacks, exchanges are also the target of cybercriminals looking to make some easy money. When it comes to hacking an exchange, the main objective here is to hijack coin or divert coin in a transaction while avoiding the corresponding payment.

This is where the fraud takes place.

Hackers just want the coin. They could care less about making the payment that is due on the value of the coin. So, they can pose as real investors. In that regard, real investors engage in the trade unbeknownst of the true intentions behind the fraudster. The transaction takes place as the coins change hands, but the counterpart of the transaction does not. So, the investor is defrauded as they do not receive the corresponding payment. Then, the fraudsters disappear with the coin.

A lot of times, hackers will gain illegal access to an existing user's accounts. So, it's not like they can just long on the system as a brand-new user. In fact, hackers circle the internet like sharks hoping to find an unsuspecting victim. When they do, they can steal their login credentials.

This is why coin exchanges take precautions to ensure that they aren't being taken to the cleaners by cybercriminals. This also provides users the assurance that the transactions they are conducting are legit and not subject to the risk of being hacked by criminals.

Preventing Hacks

As a regular user, preventing a hack is really a matter of safeguarding your information. This generally means not sharing any kind of personal information online while also protecting the most valuable part of your account, that is, your password.

One of the most common ways that hackers like to gain access to personal information is through a scheme known as "phishing." In phishing, hackers literally cast a wide net by sending out mass emails, pretending to be a legitimate company that does business with its customers.

When customers receive "official" emails from the coin exchange, they either share the information that is requested in the email or click on the links provided in the email. This prompts the user to follow the hacker's website. Now, the hackers don't actually store any of the information on the site itself. All the page does is track keystrokes. That's how they steal your username and password. Then, they use that to go on the real site and perpetrate the crime.

Another way in which hackers gain access is through the use of malware. This generally happens when you install a virus on your computer. The virus logs keystrokes, thus causing you to unknowingly share your information with the hackers. Then, they log into your account and use it to defraud the exchange.

To prevent something like this from happening, it's important to always be suspicious of any emails that come from the exchange or any type of communication that simulates the exchange. If you are prompted to change your password by email, this is a red flag. When you are prompted to change your password because it has expired, this will happen when you actually log on to the site.

Another way in which you can prevent your information from being stolen is to avoid logging into your account(s) while you are on a public WiFi network. In this "hotpots," hackers can set up a system to intercept the flow of data traffic. As a result, they can catch information such as passwords and usernames, along with credit card information, social security numbers, and so on.

Also, if there are multiple individuals using one computer, it's best to avoid using it for your account management. By entering your information on a shared computer, you are creating an unnecessary vulnerability. This is why it's always a good idea to conduct your business on a computer that you know is completely safe.

Lastly, there is your phone. If you are planning on using your phone, even just to check your account, make sure you set up some kind of authentication. This could be something like fingerprint or face recognition ID. This could save your accounts in case your phone is lost or stolen. Many times, unscrupulous individuals steal phones, not for the phone itself, but for the information they can access. If you have a fingerprint or face ID enabled function, it is impossible for hackers to gain. They would have to literally destroy the phone in the attempt to bypass these security features.

As you can see, playing it safe goes a long way when it comes to protecting your account and data. So, do make a habit of adopting preventive measures. It can save your account while protecting the users on exchanges. This will allow you to have a great experience trading crypto while ensuring the market remains safe. All you need is some rather basic security habits. Ultimately, you have control of your accounts and your coins.

CHAPTER 8

Fundamental Computer Analysis

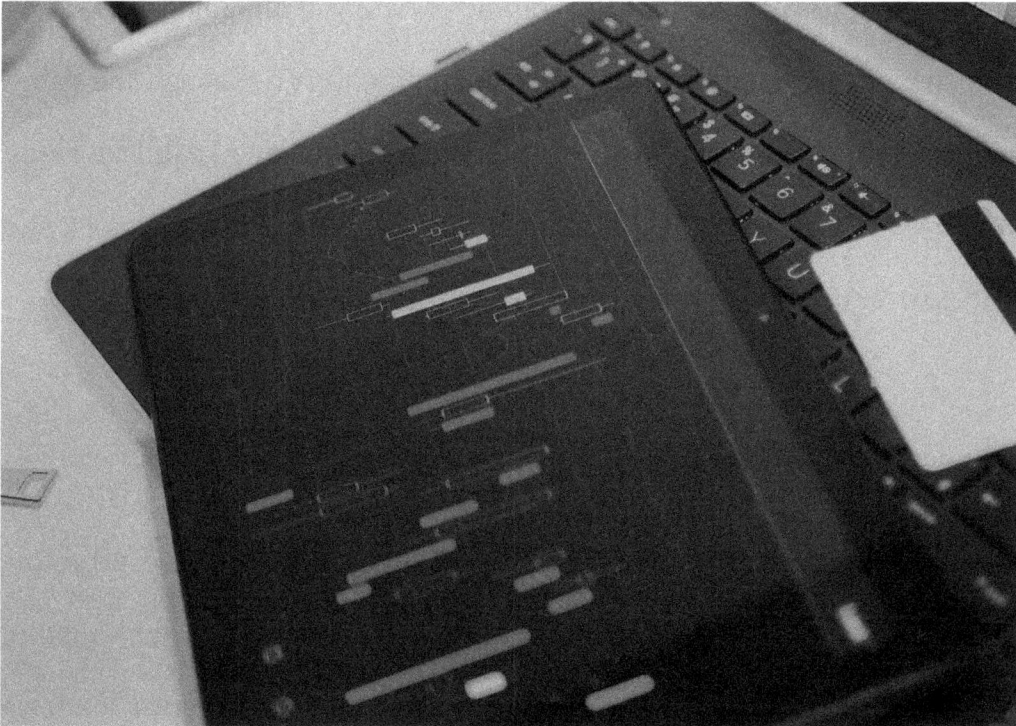

In this chapter, we are going to be looking at the ways in which you can utilize technical analysis tools and techniques to identify price action and thereby set up your trades effectively. So, please don't let the name throw you off. We're not going to be focusing on coding or programming. We're going to be focusing on data analysis methods. This will enable you to further develop your skills and understand with regard to trading cryptos.

The term "computer analysis" refers to the fact that we are using software tools to analyze the quantitative data generated by the price action of the coins you are tracking. This is important to note as we are not going to be crunching the numbers by hand. Of course, you could totally do it if you wanted to, but it's much better if you decided to use computer software programs to manage these data.

Also, it's important to consider that the volume of data you are going to be looking at is quite extensive. So, it would be quite time-consuming to run through the data without using computer-aided tools. This makes it imperative for you to take full advantage of the tools you have at your disposal. If you are unfamiliar with some of these tools, please take the time to go over them so that you can feel comfortable utilizing them.

Indicators for Coin Analysis

Throughout this book, we have discussed a number of indicators. These indicators can be used to help you make an assessment of the conditions surrounding the valuation of the coin itself. When you go about analyzing the overall conditions referring to the valuation of a coin, there are a number of issues that you need to take into account. So, we'll briefly go over some of the items we have already discussed while considering additional elements.

1. **Price**. Price is the most common indicator. This is the clearest indicator regarding the valuation of a coin. When you look at price, you see what the market thinks the valuation of the coin should be. Now, there are two things to consider here. First, if there is a large supply of a coin, then the price would tend to be lower. The other factor

is investor perception regarding the potential of a coin. This is a highly subjective assessment with regard to the potential demand for the coin.

2. **Trend**. We have discussed trend quite extensively. So, it's worth mentioning at this point that if the trend surrounding a crypto is predominantly bullish, then you can infer that the valuation of a currency will increase over time.

3. **Average**. When considering average, it's important to see how average prices play over a given time period. If you choose to plot a chart using only average prices, you can get a good idea of what the overall price action is like. This is where you can use the moving average indicator to make an assessment regarding the overall price action. Furthermore, charts displaying candlesticks will help you get a good sense of the opening and closing price throughout a given period.

4. **Trading volume**. Trading volume is a highly useful indicator that can help you to assess the overall amount of transactions during a given period. This is the reflection of the "popularity" of a coin. Those coins which have a higher trading volume reflect greater interest on the part of investors.

5. **Cross rates**. This is a term borrowed from FOREX. A Cross rate refers to the valuation of a coin based on different currencies or other cryptos. For example, Bitcoin is valued in US Dollars, Euros, or other cryptos like Litecoin or Ethereum. When you compare the various cross rates, you can make an assessment according to the overall valuation of a

coin. If you find that the price of Bitcoin is much higher in Litecoin than Ethereum, it could be that Litecoin is undervalued. This would reveal a lot more about Litecoin that it does about Bitcoin.

Please bear in mind that the crypto space hasn't been around for quite as long as other markets. So, this implies that the number of indicators available isn't quite as broad as other markets. This is a sign of maturity. When you have markets that have been around for a while, you will find that there are a larger number of indicators available. This is a reflection of how investors and analysts develop their own indicators to help make a better assessment. Consequently, you can expect the scope of indicators available in the crypto space will grow over time.

Ichimoku Cloud

The Ichimoku Cloud is a technical analysis tool that compares various measures at once. It is used to show support and resistance levels based on available data sets. It is intended to provide further insight into price action information beyond the traditional candlestick chart or trendline analysis. As such, this chart groups a number of indicators so that their analysis in unison provides a greater data set. The cross-referencing of the various data points enables investors and analysts to make more informed decisions into entry and exit points.

This tool can be used with stocks, FOREX, and commodities. Therefore, it is perfectly applicable to the world of crypto. All you need is the corresponding data to make the set work. These charts can be generated by the information service available on your trading platform. These charts are generated automatically by simply overlaying the various indicators in a single chart.

The basis for the Ichimoku Cloud is the traditional candlestick chart that plots price action over a given timeframe. Since the data represented on the candlestick chart itself is rather limited, the Ichimoku Cloud looks to augment this information. Thus, moving average indicators are used to supplement the information contained in this chart. Consequently, the 26-period and the 52-period moving average are overlaid.

When you hear the term "26-period" moving average, the word "period" refers to the specific time periods analyzed as part of the chart. Generally speaking, a period in this sense of the word refers to hours. Of course, the period could be longer, depending on the type of asset you are analyzing. For example, stocks use the 20-day moving average. This means that price action is tracked over days and not hours. However, the FOREX market, which is much more dynamic than stocks, uses hourly periods to track price action. As such, you are looking at a timeframe of about 24 to 48 hours, meaning roughly two days of action.

There are five parts that need to be calculated to make the Ichimoku Cloud:

- Conversion line

- Base line

- Leading Span A

- Leading Span B

- Lagging Span

These elements are what create the cloud in the graph. When you trace the cloud, you end up getting the predictive measure of what you can expect down the road. As such, the Ichimoku Cloud is quite good at enabling you to predict future support and resistance levels based on available information. Plus, you can spot where potential reversals may occur.

In its calculation, you are essentially taking the high and low prices of the 26-periods. This enables you to calculate the leading span, which seeks to determine price action 26 periods into the future. The leading span A is based on the high while leading span B is based on the low price. Once you have this setup, you will see a green cloud and a red one. The green cloud indicates prices above the average while the red cloud indicates prices below the average.

On its own, the Ichimoku Cloud is generally used as a means of confirming resistance and support levels. Consequently, you can pair this indicator with a simple overlay of the moving average along with other technical analysis indicators such as trend, trading volume, and others such as the Relative Strength Index (RSI). The RSI is used to evaluate an asset is being overbought or oversold. Thus, you can use the RSI to confirm any assumptions you may have about a coin's overall momentum. It could be that price action is reacting to an oversold condition or hasn't yet reacted to an overbought condition. Either way, the RSI, along with other indicators, can serve to create a solid technical analysis foundation for your assessments.

The biggest drawback of the Ichimoku Cloud is that the chart is filled with a great deal of information on it. At first glance, it can be quite overwhelming. Thus, you can use charting software to hide certain lines. This allows you to analyze the entire chart in individual segments. Then, you can look at the entire action to see the interaction of all the data.

In addition, the Ichimoku Cloud is based on historical information. This means that you are taking previous price action to project into the future. While this is a perfectly valid statistical model, the fact that you are basing your predictions on a short timeframe means that you won't be able to project very far into the future. If you choose to look at longer data sets to overcome this situation, you will find that its predictive capabilities are quite limited. This is why the Ichimoku Cloud should always be paired with other indicators in order to obtain a broader picture of the price action.

Oscillators

Oscillators are used as a part of technical analysis tools to determine trend and momentum. In the world of FOREX, oscillators are quite commonly used to make a predictive analysis. Now, it should be noted that oscillators don't study trend; as such, rather they study "momentum." Momentum refers to the condition of being overbought or oversold.

When discussing the RSI, we mentioned these two conditions. The reason why they are relevant is due to the fact that trading volume will indicate if an asset is being predominantly bought or predominantly sold. This is important to take into account as either condition will generate momentum in one direction or another.

Hence, trend refers specifically to price action, while momentum refers to the trading volume, that is, the specific amount of "buy" or "sell" transactions.

On the surface, when an asset is oversold, it means that holders are getting rid of their positions. This would imply a potential fall in price. On the other hand, when an asset is being overbought, this means that investors are looking to acquire as much as they can. Therefore, you can assume that price will move up based on increased demand.

Additionally, when an asset is being oversold, you can infer that its price is overvalued. This means that holders assume that the price is higher than expected and thus would like to sell before it falls. Also, when an asset is being overbought, investors feel that it is undervalued and thus want to scoop it up before price increases.

This is why the use of oscillators helps you determine if you are dealing with a coin that is actually under or overvalued.

If you are looking to purchase, and overbought coin means that the market feels it is undervalued. As a result, you could consider getting in. By the same token, if you are holding a coin and see an oversold condition, that is an indication that it's time to liquidate your position before price plunges.

The easiest way to calculate oscillation is to take the current price and subtract it from the previous price. This simple formula implies that if you get a positive value, then momentum is increasing as price is gaining. If the result is negative, then this implies that price is falling, and momentum is negative.

The current price used in this calculation is based on the specific moment you are analyzing, for instance, at this very moment. The previous price is rather subjective. You can choose to compare price action on an hourly basis. So, if it's currently 11 am, you can subtract the 11 am price from the 10 am price. You can do this as far back as you like though the industry standard as an hour by hour basis.

Another commonly-used oscillator is known as the stochastic oscillator. The term "stochastic" is a statistical term used to refer to randomness. So, this oscillator looks to determine if there is randomness in the price action you are analyzing. This is important as randomness would be indicative of market forces outside of the traditional patterns which you may have observed. Randomness may be the result of unforeseen events that are putting pressure on the market as opposed to investor expectations and psyche.

Stochastic oscillators are used to determine buy and sell signals. This oscillator can be used in conjunction with the moving average and RSI to provide further indication of trend reversals and divergences that may occur in pricing. As such, you can use this oscillator to establish if there is a high or low degree in the randomness associated with the price action you are analyzing.

Alligators

Alligators are commonly used in the world of FOREX to determine if there are trends forming or to establish the absence of one. When a trend is under formation, the alligator can tell you which direction it is going. If there is no trend, then the alligator will confirm this.

The reason why this indicator is called an alligator has to do with the behavior of trend. So, it's not that the charting action resembles an alligator in any way. Rather, it's the behavior that resembles an alligator's behavior.

This analogy is based on the fact that an absence of trend, that is a sideways or horizontal trendline, resembles a sleeping alligator. However, there is a point in which the alligator must wake up. When the alligator wakes up, it will be hungry and in search of prey. The premise is that the longer the alligator sleeps, the hungrier it will be. This means that once the sideways trend is broken, the new trend, bearish or bullish, will be considerably sharper.

The alligator formation is composed of three separate moving averages. These are called "balance lines." When these lines are compared, you can determine if the sideways trend will be bearish or bullish. Most importantly, you can also determine how sharp it will be.

The first line is called the alligator's jaw. This is generally marked in blue, and it is composed of a 13-period moving average. It is then moved forward by an additional 8 candlesticks (21 periods in total).

The second line is called the alligator's teeth. This line is represented in red. This is the moving average of eight periods, then moved forward and an additional 5 (13 candlesticks total).

The third line is called the alligator's lips. This line is shown in green. It is the 5- period moving average and then moved 3 candlesticks forward (8 in total).

The comparison of these three lines tells you where the trend will likely end up at any given point. The absence of trend can be spotted when the three lines are very closed bunched up together. The closer they stick together, the greater the absence of trend. The alligator wakes up when the green line crosses over the other two. Since the green line is the fastest moving average, it indicates the momentum of trend formation. If its spike is noticeably sharper than the other two, then this indicates the level of hunger in the alligator. As such, the divergence of the green line in comparison with the other two indicates how pronounced the new trend will be.

Perhaps the most difficult aspect of the alligator pattern is to identify the exact moment when the break in horizontal trend will happen. So, it's a matter of keeping a close eye on potential crossovers. This is the clearest indicator of when the break in sideways trend will actually occur.

Japanese Candlestick Patterns

In this pattern, we are going to be looking exclusively at candlesticks and the patterns they represent. Consequently, we will be discussing how you can read candlesticks effectively as part of your overall research task.

It should be noted that we are going to use a simple candlestick chart. As such, we are not going to be using any other statistical indicators beyond candlesticks. However, you might think they are simply candlesticks; what they reveal is far more telling.

Please bear in mind that a candlestick measures the following: the high price, the low price, and the spread among the opening and closing price. As such, the candlestick's body represents the spread between the opening and closing price with the upper line represents the high price, and the lower line represents the low price. Additionally, when the body of the stick is black, it indicates that the closing price was lower than the opening. When the stick is white (or transparent), it indicates that the closing price was higher than the opening.

This is where the various Japanese interpretations of the candlesticks come into play. They represent the various ways in which the sticks can tell you what to expect from the information seen in the chart. This can help you to figure out where the momentum is going at any given time.

The Spinning Top

The first configuration to look at is called a "spinning top." This configuration is highlighted by a narrow (or short) candlestick body. The color is essentially meaningless, while the high and low price are exactly the same (or very close to being exactly the same). This configuration indicates a high degree of indecision among investors. Essentially, it means that there were no "winners" or "losers" in that period; everyone broke even, so to speak.

There are two possible interpretations of a spinning top. If there is a spinning top during an upward trend, it could signal that there aren't that many buyers left. This is a signal for a potential reversal to a downward trend. On the other hand, if a spinning top is present in a downward trend, it indicates that there aren't that many sellers left in the market. As such, it signals a potential reversal to an upward trend.

The Marubozu Candlestick

The "Marubozu" stick (which literally means "bald" in Japanese) indicates the stick has no "shadow." This means that the upper and lower lines are non-existent. What that means is that the high and low price are exactly the same.

There are two types of Marubozu. A white Marubozu means that the opening price equals the low price, and the close price equals the price. Consequently, the stick is white, but the shadows are gone. In contrast, a black Marubozu means that the opening price equals the high price and the closing price is the same as the low price. Therefore, you can interpret that the asset lost in value.

Here are the possible interpretations of a Marubozu:

The emergence of a white Marubozu at the end of an upward trend signals that a continuation of the trend is likely. If you spot a white Marubozu at the end of a downward trend, then a reversal is likely.

The emergence of a black Marubozu at the end of a downward trend means the trend is likely to continue. If you see a black Marubozu at the end of an upward trend, then a reversal is likely to happen.

The Marubozu candlesticks are great at spotting potential trend reversals or continuations, particularly if you are following resistance levels and trendlines. If you spot these sticks at points in which resistance and support levels are going to intersect with a trendline, then you definitely have the confirmation you need to make your assessments accurately.

The Doji Candlesticks

Doji candlesticks are used to measure the struggle between buyers and sellers. In essence, you are looking at the turf war that may emerge between the two as the jockey for position in a market. The Doji can also represent indecision, especially when there is a great deal of uncertainty surrounding a market.

The easiest way to identify a Doji candlestick is by the very narrow body. So, you have the upper and lower shadows with a very thin body that basically resembles a straight line. This means that neither buyers nor sellers were able to really make any kind of headway during that particular time. If you happen to spot these sticks, then you are in for one of four possible configurations.

1. **Long-legged Doji**. This is akin to a perfectly centered cross. The upper and lower shadows are the same length, while a very narrow body slices both lines right through the middle. This indicates a high degree of indecision as neither buyers nor sellers were able to come out ahead.

2. **Dragonfly Doji**. This candlestick has practically no upper shadow with the narrow body all the way to the top while a very long lower body is visible. This configuration is generally seen at the point of a possible reversal as the asset's open, close and high prices are the same. The trend reversal could go either way, so it is neither bearish nor bullish.

3. **Gravestone Doji.** This configuration is the opposite of the Dragonfly. This stick has a long upper shadow while the lower shadow is quite short. The narrow body is located at the

bottom of the stick. This is generally a bearish sign that indicates a potential reversal. In this stick, the open, close, and low price are all the same.

4. **Four price Doji.** In this stick, all four prices open, close, high, and low are exactly the same, or very close to it. Therefore, the stick just has the narrow, horizontal body with no visible upper and lower shadow. This candlestick indicates the highest possible level of indecision in the market. It is generally seen at the very top or very bottom of a trend. It is usually the confirmation of the uppermost or lowermost point. Thus, the next stick would indicate the official beginning of the new trend.

When you are dealing with Doji, you need to be certain about the preceding sticks. This will serve to understand where trend is heading and where you can expect it to move going forward. Consequently, these sticks cannot be interpreted in isolation. They need to be seen within the context of the entire time period you are analyzing.

In general, you can interpret Doji in the following manner:

If you see a Doji following a series of black Marobozu, then the Doji indicates that sellers are beginning to grow tired. This means that there are fewer and fewer sellers. In order for the falling price to continue, more sellers would be needed in the market. But since sellers are basically exhausted, buyers will soon flood the market, triggering a reversal in trend. The confirmation of the trend reversal would be a white Marubozu. This would be a great time to buy.

The opposite scenario is also true. If you spot a Doji following a series of white Marubozu, then what you have is a series of buyers become exhausted. This means that the number of investors interested in purchasing is becoming lower. Therefore, the Doji would indicate the point in which asset holders are ready to begin selling. This would mean falling prices as the market becomes flooded with supply. This would be the ideal time to sell. The confirmation of the new trend would be represented by a black Marubozu. If you haven't already liquidated your position by then, you should consider selling before your profits begin to shrink.

Japanese sticks are not to be taken as the sole indicator of a reversal or continuation of trend. If you spot these in addition to the other indicators that we have outlined throughout this book, you will find a very good indication of the patterns that you seek. Therefore, you can plan your strategy accordingly. It's also important to use Japanese sticks as a means of confirming your overall assessment of price action. You will find that Japanese sticks are a great way of confirming what you have already been able to spot at plain sight.

Cryptocurrency Market Regulations

One of the biggest aspects of the crypto space is regulation. Given the fact that cryptos are rather new, there are many aspects that users and investors might be unsure about. Therefore, it's important to do some research in order to understand what regulation applies to the crypto space and how you can take advantage of it.

In this section, we are going to look at how the crypto market is regulated, or unregulated, and how you can use that to your advantage. As a disclaimer, please ensure that you get any legal advice from a licensed professional. In this manner, you can avoid committing any illegal action inadvertently. The last thing that we want is for you to accidentally engage in any activity that might be construed as illegal. Thus, always make sure that you seek the proper legal counsel whenever you are in doubt.

Crypto Regulation

Crypto regulation is scant at best. Only a handful of countries around the world have specific regulations regarding cryptocurrencies. This basically means that cryptos are not illegal, but it also means they aren't legal, either.

One of the aspects which are perfectly clear is that no country recognizes any crypto as legal tender. This means that cryptos may be used to settle private accounts among individuals. However, the use of cryptos does not constitute a legally binding agreement. In a manner of speaking, it's like swapping goods. This would not constitute a legal purchase as money legal tender was exchanged. Therefore, the seller cannot claim any benefit from the sale, while the buyer cannot claim they were defrauded in any way.

Perhaps the biggest concern when it comes to regulation in the crypto market is the issue of paying taxes. Depending on the country where you live, you might be on the hook for taxes based on the gains you make. Now, it should be noted that very few countries tax cryptos as assets. For instance, Israel considers cryptos to be assets. As such, holders are liable to pay taxes on them. Similarly, Bulgaria taxes cryptos as assets. This means that holders would pay a tax similar to what homeowners pay their property.

In other countries, profits made on the trade of cryptos are taxed. For instance, Argentina and Spain tax cryptos as part of an individual's income tax. Switzerland taxes cryptos as they would foreign currency. In the UK, individuals pay capital gains tax on any profits made from trading cryptos.

As you can see, the various ways in which countries regulate cryptos for fiscal purposes is rather broad. In the United States, cryptos are not subject to any taxation. However, the gains made from the trading of cryptos are. So, it's always best to double-check with your local state for any sales tax on cryptos while it's also important to double-check any applicable federal taxes that might be applicable. At the time of writing, crypto traders are only subject to capital gains tax. This means that making money on cryptos is taxed much in the same way the gains on the sale of a house would be.

Crypto Deregulation

It should be noted that the lack of regulation within the crypto space is actually an advantage when you consider the vast amount of regulation in the stock and commodities markets. Therefore, trading cryptos is largely up to the individuals who engage in trading them.

In essence, if you bought a bunch of coins, you are basically up to whatever the market dictates them t be worth. In a manner of speaking, it's like buying a car. The government cannot regulate what a car is worth. This is entirely up to the market.

Detractors of the crypto market claim that the lack of government oversight makes it inherently dangerous to trade in this space. They claim that there are no consumer protections in place. Therefore, if you happen to get fleeced or defrauded in a deal, there is nothing you can do. While criminal charges may apply as far as the scam itself, there is nothing that can regulate the trade of cryptos themselves.

On the other hand, supporters of the crypto space highlight this to be one of the best aspects of cryptocurrencies. Since these are meant to be decentralized, there is a clear intent to ensure that there is little government interference.

While it is true that having legal backing makes transactions safer and easier to manage, it should also be noted that too much government interference tends to make markets rather inefficient. If you are seriously looking into the possibility of buying and selling cryptos, the best way to manage this is to ensure that you are dealing with reputable companies and individuals. Any backdoor deals are almost always a sign of trouble.

This is why any underground markets and exchanges are best avoided. And yes, it is true that there are illegal transactions conducted in cryptocurrency. This is why you want to avoid any shady characters as much as possible. It could very well be that you end up getting mixed up with the wrong crowd.

Beyond that, the crypto space offers a great deal of opportunity for up-and-coming investors. Cryptos are here to stay. So, it's a question of understanding the market and knowing where to place your chips. If done right, you can make a fortune in the crypto space. At worst, you can make modest returns that are good enough to supplement your income. Of course, it's always a good idea to keep your eye on the price. Who knows, you may get in on the next Bitcoin right from the start. That certainly sounds like something to look forward to. There is plenty of room for growth. This is just the beginning of the future.

CHAPTER 9

Cryptotrading Psychology

Investors from all walks of life have varying types of mindsets. These mindsets can be conservative or openly aggressive. While these are the extremes, so to speak, it's important to consider that you don't have to conform to a specific type of mindset in order to be successful. You just have to learn how to manage your own mindset so that you can set yourself up to be successful.

In this regard, making money in cryptotrading is a combination of technical skills and good instincts. When you combine both aspects correctly, you can develop a discipline that will set you up for success at all points throughout your trading endeavors. If you are unable to manage the psychological aspects that come with trading, then you might find yourself in a disadvantageous position.

This is why this chapter is dedicated to analyzing the mindset of a successful cryptotrader and how you can adopt the best traits. Most important, you will find that these traits do not require you to overhaul your personality. All it requires is for you to manage your mindset in such a way that you are making the right kind of choices based on the information you have available.

Best of all, you will find that being cognizant of the weaknesses in your own mindset will help develop a long-term approach that can translate into other types of investments beyond cryptos. In the end, you could be setting up what might be a long and prosperous trading career.

The Typical Cryptotrading Mindset

The "typical" mindset is to make as much money as possible. Plain and simple. This is what all investors seek. After all, no one goes into investing thinking to lose money. Thus, it's important to consider the role that expectations play.

When the average individual goes into any kind of investment (not just cryptos), they may build unrealistic expectations in their mind. They might think they are going to clean up and become rich overnight. They may even buy into the false promises made by some companies that purport easy money-making schemes.

These are the ads you really need to be careful with.

Sure, it's not hard to make money in cryptos. However, you need to know what you are doing. That's what this book is all about. Part of that knowledge and understanding is realizing that you won't become rich overnight. Of course, you could make some decent money in a short period of time. But then again, it takes time and effort to build the type of portfolio that will guarantee you a good quality of life.

This is why novice investors ought to look at this type of investment as a means of supplementing their income. In the end, this supplemental income can serve to pay bills, cut down on debt, or save up for larger expenses such as a new car or a down payment on a home.

If you believe the stories that some so-called experts use to sell their gimmicks, then it's best you gave these stories further thought. The fact is that get-rich-quick schemes deliver underwhelming results in the best of cases.

Consequently, the "typical" mindset is based on high hopes or unrealistic expectations. In fact, you'll find that some novice investors get into cryptos, FOREX, or stocks in the hopes of suddenly quitting their job and living a fancy lifestyle filled with travel and exotic quirks.

This could not be farther from the truth.

The most successful investors spend the bulk of their time studying the markets and planning their next moves. They spend a great deal of their attention, looking at how to improve their investment strategy. This is what leads them to be the successful investors that they are.

Now, we're not saying that you should give up your regular life and immerse yourself full-time into graphs and charts. What we are saying is that living a lavish lifestyle is usually the result of hard work and dedication to investing. Additionally, your goal should not be to quit your day job. Your ultimate goal should be to build up enough revenue streams so that you don't have to depend on just one source of income.
This is what true financial independence is all about.

When you don't depend on your paycheck or the gains you make trading, you can truly become free of the rat race. Once you have the ability to choose what to do with your time and your efforts, you have the ability to truly live the life that you want to live.

Now that certainly sounds like something great, doesn't it?

The fact is that what we all aspire is to become free of debt and have the luxury to take time off, travel, or just spend time with our loved ones. This is the underlying idea behind investing. It's not just about making money for the sake of making money. It's about finding what you truly want out of life.

The Successful Cryptotrading Mindset

A successful mindset boils down to your ability to manage your expectations while putting in the time and effort needed to become a successful investor. This is the main objective. Developing the skills you need to become a successful investor will enable you to grow both in terms of your knowledge as well as your experience.

With that in mind, here are some helpful tips which will allow you to develop a discipline that will ensure your success at all points of your trading career.

1. **Set a realistic target.** Firstly, think about how much money you could reasonably make at the outset of your trading career. This could be something as simple as two or three hundred dollars. Yet, understanding that at least you'd be turning a profit from the first week you are trading ought to be enough to keep you motivated. In reality, it all boils down to your investment capital. If you invest thousands per trade, you could make a good deal of money. But if you start out with a few hundred dollars, then you need to work your way up. It will take some time, but you will get there. By keeping your eyes on the prize, you'll get there very soon.

2. **Reinvest only a part of your winnings**. Some investors like to sink all of their profits back into investing. Sure, this is a great way to make your investment capital grow quickly. However, it's not always the best way to go about managing your money. This is why you should only reinvest a part of your money. The rest of the money should go toward things that you need to pay off or even a small luxury. Even if it's just going to dinner on a Friday night, spending some of your earnings on yourself will go a long way.

3. **Set up a schedule**. While you shouldn't look at trading as if it were an obligation, it's always a good idea to set up a schedule. This builds a routine that will help you stay focused on your goals. When you trade in your "free time," you'll find that you are rather inconsistent. When this happens, it's tough to build momentum. As you build momentum through a series of successful trades, you will need to keep moving forward at a consistent pace. Otherwise, you'll let your success cool off. By the same token, if you fall into a losing streak, you have a greater chance of breaking it by being consistent as opposed to "taking time off."

4. **Don't dwell on the past.** Whether you win or lose, it's best to let go of the past. When you have a hot streak, you might get caught up in your own success. You might think that you have everything down, and there is no need for further study or research. This may lead to a false sense of security. Needless to say, it is not a good place to be. If you happen to fall into a cold streak, you might be down and upset with yourself. If you dwell on negative experiences for too long, you'll end up killing any interest you may

have in investing. This is why you need to let go of the past and focus on what's coming up ahead. This is how you can truly develop laser-sharp focus.

5. **Celebrate both wins and losses.** Celebrating wins is easy. You high-five everyone and brag about your accomplishments. That's all well and fine. However, you should also celebrate defeat as each loss leaves you with a valuable lesson. If you take losses in stride, you'll end up learning so much. This is the type of knowledge you can't buy with money. It's like becoming battle-tested. No amount of courses and training can give you combat experience. As you gain that experience, you'll be able to truly focus on your life and what you have to gain.

With these insights, you will develop a strong mindset that will be impossible to break down. Over time, you will develop the skills and discipline that you need to become a successful investor. So, there is nowhere to go but up!

CHAPTER 10

Glossary Of Basic Cryptocurrency Terms

- Altcoin

This term is a combination of the words "alternative" and "coin." As such, "altcoin" refers to any cryptocurrency that is an alternative to Bitcoin. Therefore, this term includes virtually all cryptos except Bitcoin.

- ASIC

Acronym for the Australian Securities & Investment Commission. This is the government organization that oversees trading of financial assets and securities.

- Bears

"Bears" refers to a pessimistic view of the market and trends. Any time an asset loses value or the market is in a downward situation, the term "bearish" is used.

- Bitcoin

A cryptocurrency consisting of a digital token that can be used to settle accounts and facilitate commercial transactions. It is the most popular cryptocurrency and the most valuable.

- itcoin address

A digital address which serves as the destination for a payment in Bitcoin. It is an alphanumeric code consisting of 26-35 characters. It generally begins with the numbers 1, 3, or BC1. Additionally, a dedicated wallet can also serve as a destination for a payment issued in Bitcoin.

- Bitcoin cash

A spinoff crypto of the traditional Bitcoin cryptocurrency. It was launched in 2017. Since then, it has been split up into Bitcoin Cash and Bitcoin SV.

- Bitcoin Wallet

Digital repository where digital Bitcoin tokens are stored. It can be an individual vault service or an exchange such as Coinbase.

- Blockchain

Digital ledger technology on which cryptocurrencies are built upon. It is used to verify transactions and create transparency among users.

- Bulls

This term is used any time optimistic expectations are set regarding a market, asset, or individual security. When investors are optimistic about an asset, they are said to be "bullish." When trend is "bullish," it refers to increasing price action.

- Cloud Mining

Internet-based computer power used to generate a digital token of any crypto. Dedicated datacenters are used to serve as the underlying computing power for blockchain technology. In exchange, these datacenters receive a digital token, which can later be traded for a profit.

- Crowdsale

A "crowdsale" is a public online event in which participants purchase digital cryptocurrency tokens. This event is akin to an auction. Buyers and sellers meet to swap coins or cryptos for legal tender.

- Dump

A quick sale of an asset usually the result of a sudden drop in price. To "dump" an asset means to sell as soon as possible, often below the expected price. The main point is to exit a position before the price falls into red territory.

- Ethereum

An altcoin. It is a blockchain that produces a cryptocurrency called "Ether," which can be used to settle accounts and facilitate payments. It is a common alternative to Bitcoin or Litecoin.

- Farm

Process in which dedicate computing power looks to generate cryptocurrency tokens. It is also referred to as "mining." In this process, computers are dedicated to conducting the processes outlined by the specific blockchain in order to produce token. These tokens can then be resold for a profit.

- Fiat

The term used to refer to legal tender as issued by a sovereign government. The word "fiat" refers to "decree," that is, the currency derives its value from a government decree and not by any characteristics which give it value as is the case of gold.

- Fork

This term is used to refer to the action in which a crypto is split into two separate coins. This can be done to increase its supply or to dedicate part of one blockchain to a different type of process. A common example of this is the fork created from Bitcoin. Bitcoin was split up into Bitcoin Cash and Bitcoin SV. All three are separate coins though they share the same blockchain technology.

- ICO

An acronym which refers to an "initial coin offering." Some coin issuers would rather launch a set number of coins into the market as opposed to mining them. ICOs can be purchased by investors much in the same way companies issues their IPOs (initial public offering).

- Litecoin

An altcoin. Litecoin is used as an alternative to Bitcoin. It is in the same ballpark as Ethereum. It can be used to settle accounts or facilitate commercial transactions.

- Market Depth

The amount of cryptocurrency supply for a specific coin or group of coins. It also refers to the overall supply in the market.

- Masternode (Proof of Stake)

A computer, or network of computer which combines its power, used to ensure the integrity of a coin network. In essence, a masternode is a computer system that houses a crypto's full ledger history as opposed to having the ledger history split up into various computer systems.

- Miner

Person or organization dedicated to the production of cryptocurrency tokens. Also known as a "farmer."

- Mining

Process in which dedicate computing power looks to generate cryptocurrency tokens. It is also referred to as "farming." In this process, computers are dedicated to conducting the processes outlined by the specific blockchain in order to produce tokens. These tokens can then be resold for a profit.

- Network complexity

This term refers to the level of sophistication that is involved in setting up a computer network either as part of the blockchain or the digital ledger. It can also refer to the process of mining or farming for coins.

- Order

The action of placing a trade. There are two types of orders, "buy" and "sell."

- Peak

A spike in price which leads to a high point in price. A peak usually signals an increase in overall price trend.

- Pending

A transaction that has not been completed until certain conditions are met such a target price or timeframe.

- Pool

The action of "pooling" the resources of various miners in order to increase computing power, thereby enabling greater capacity for generating crypto tokens.

- PoS Mining (Proof of Stake)

The process in which individuals verify transactions on a blockchain. The Proof of Stake process validates a transaction, thereby leading to the generation of a digital token.

- Pump

The action in which the price is driven up as a result of increased demand. When price is pumped up, it can surpass previous highs.

- Satoshi

Purported pseudonym used by the creators of Bitcoin blockchain technology.

- Swing

A term referring to the fluctuations in market prices. It also refers to changes in trend as observed by reversals from bearish to bullish and so on.

- Tokens

Digital coins which make up a cryptocurrency.

- Transaction

Action in which two sides come to an agreement. There is usually an exchange of some sort. The transaction can be finalized either by the use of legal tender or a cryptocurrency.

CONCLUSION

Thank you for making it to the end of this volume. We hope that the information you found herein has been helpful in your discovery of cryptocurrencies and how you can invest in this exciting new market.

By now, you have everything you need to get started investing in cryptos. Best of all, the entire process has been rather straightforward. As such, there are no complex processes or the need for advanced college degrees.

Making money in cryptos is a combination of both savvy and perseverance. When you are able to combine these elements, you will find that making money as an investor in this field is not nearly as hard as you might have thought.

So, what's next?

Well, the time has come to get to work. Please do your homework into crypto exchange, which offers you the support you need in order to get started in this dynamic market. Most importantly, please look for an exchange which can offer you the security measures you need in order to ensure that your coins are kept nice and safe.

Given the fact that the crypto space is a rather new market, you have the opportunity to get in now, while most investors are still unfamiliar with the concept of making profits through the trade of digital tokens.

So, what are you waiting for?

Go on and get started today. When you realize just how much money you can make trading cryptos, you will regret not having gotten into it sooner.

Thanks again for taking the time to read this book. If you have found it to be useful and informative, do leave a comment so that other readers can discover the value which you have found herein. And by all means, tell your friends, family, and colleagues about this book if you feel they too will benefit from it.

Happy trading!

www.ingramcontent.com/pod-product-compliance
Lightning Source LLC
Chambersburg PA
CBHW081807200326
41597CB00023B/4181